David McIntosh & Arturo E. Beéche

Royal Exiles in Cannes

The Bourbons of the Two Sicilies
of the Villa Marie-Thérèse

ISBN: 978-0-9854603-8-9

EUROHISTORY.COM

EUROHISTORY.COM

6300 Kensington Avenue
East Richmond Heights, CA 94805 USA
Phone: (510) 236-1730 – Email: books@eurohistory.com

Royal Exiles in Cannes
The Bourbons of the Two Sicilies of the Villa Marie-Thérèse
©David McIntosh & Arturo E. Beéche

ISBN: 978-0-9854603-8-9

Artistic Design ©Arturo Beéche & David W. Higdon

The author and publisher of this book also wish to express their gratitufde to
the following individuals and entities for supplying illustrations for this publication:

HRH The Duke of Calabria, Infante of Spain & HRH The Duke of Castro
HRH The Duke of Noto & HRH The Duke of Capua
TIRH Archduke Simeon and Archduchess Maria of Austria
HRH Victoria of Bourbon-Two Sicilies, Mrs. Nomikos
HRH Princess Annunziata of Bourbon-Two Sicilies, Countess Creutz
HRH Princess Elena sofía of Bourbon-Two Sicilies
HSH The Fürstin of Isenburg
Prince Gregory de Bourbon
Ilia García de Saez
Guy Stair Sainty
Dátivo Salvia Ocaña, Kaija Jokiharu & Eric van de Vloet
The Eurohistory Royal Photo Archive
The William Mead Lalor Archive @ Eurohistory

We would like to thank our dear friend Larry Russell ...

We also wish to thank everyone else who helped us with this project, especially those who were instrumental in encouraging this book.

Other friends whose encouragement and support Eurohistory wishes to acknowledge, include:
Annet Bakker at Hoogstraten English Bookstore, Nicolas Fouint at Librairie Galignani, Joe Little and Jeannie Pittard-Whitmarsh at MAJESTY, Ted Rosvall at Rosvall Royal Books, Maria Smith (Thomson-Shore), Ian Shapiro, Ricardo Mateos Saínz de Medrano, Seth Leonard, Netty Leistra and Henry Wong.

Table of Contents

Table of Contents — i

Preface — iv

Introduction — 1

Chapter I – Ferdinando I – "Nasone" — 3

Chapter II – Francesco I — 10

Chapter III – Ferdinando II – "King Bomba" — 24

Chapter IV – Francesco II – "A Last Stand at Gaeta" — 39

Chapter V – The Count and Countess of Caserta:
Alfonso & Antonietta — 49

Chapter VI – Ferdinando – Duke of Calabria — 61

Chapter VII – Carlos – Infante of Spain — 70

Chapter VIII – Maria Immacolata – Princess Johann Georg
of Saxony — 110

Chapter IX – Maria Christina – Archduchess Peter Ferdinand
of Austria-Tuscany — 115

Chapter X – Maria Pia – Princess Luiz d'Orléans-Bragança — 122

Chapter XI – Maria Giuseppina — 132

Chapter XII – Gennaro – Count di Villa Colli — 134

Chapter XIII – Ranieri – Duke of Castro — 138

Chapter XIV – Filippo — 159

Chapter XV – Gabriele — 168

Chapter XVI – A Family Photo Album — 184

Family Tree: The Bourbons of the Two Sicilies — 186

Bibliography & Sources — 204

Index — 206

VILLA MARIE-THÉRÈSE · CANNES

Preface

*A*fter the loss of their throne in 1861, the imposing façade of the Villa Marie-Thérèse in Cannes in the South of France (pictured overleaf), harboured the Bourbons of the Two Sicilies in dignified exile for many years, and its walls, now sadly destroyed, were witnesses to decades of family events — births, christenings, birthdays, engagements, weddings and deaths, each celebrated by enormous get-togethers and gatherings.

The owners, Alfonso Count of Caserta and his wife Maria Antonietta, were the progenitors of a large family, and their countless descendants are allied by marriage with many of Europe's other Catholic Imperial and Royal Houses — the Bourbons of Spain and of Parma, the Orleans and the Bonapartes of France, the Habsburg-Lorraines of Austria and Tuscany, the Savoys of Italy, the Orleans-Bragança of Brazil, the Württembergs, the Liechtensteins, the Wittelsbachs of Bavaria, the Wettins of Saxony, with the mediatised Houses of Stolberg-Wernigerode, Waldburg-Zeil and Schönborn-Wiesentheid and with the great Polish aristocratic families of Czartoryski, Lubomirski and Zamoyski, as well as with many other noble families from France, Spain, Italy and Finland, not forgetting a Vice-President of the Republic of Ecuador!

The family continues to multiply and diversify. To all lovers of things Royal and genealogical, this book attempts to make its members, those long since departed and those still alive, better known to you.

David McIntosh
Isle of Bute, April 2015

King Carlo of Naples, future King Carlos III of Spain.

Introduction

The Kingdom of the Two Sicilies was established on December 12, 1816. However, it was a successor political entity to a kingdom that had existed since the XII century, when in 1130 Roger II, Count of Sicily, assumed the title of King of Sicily. He was the first Norman monarch of the region, his grandfather Tancred of Hauteville having been a minor nobleman in France.

The Normans, as the kingdom's first dynasty was commonly known, descended from Tancred's son, Roger I. Described by a contemporary as, *"a youth of the greatest beauty, of lofty stature, of graceful shape, most eloquent*

The Royal Palace in Naples.

in speech and cool in counsel. He was farseeing in arranging all his actions, pleasant and merry all with men; strong and brave, and furious in battle," Roger conquered vast lands in Calabria (Southern Italy) and Sicily, as well as the island of Malta. By the time of his death in 1101, he had firmly established his family as rulers of these lands, while expelling the previous Muslim emirs who had ruled for several centuries.

Roger II, who once established as monarch made Palermo his capital, achieved further conquests. There he built a magnificent palace, known as the Palace of the Normans, in which he had a wonderful chapel built. The Cappella Palatina, *"with Norman doors, Saracenic arches, Byzantine dome, and roof adorned with Arabic scripts, is perhaps the most striking product of the brilliant and mixed civilization"* over which Roger II ruled. This exquisite structure still stands proudly in Palermo, where it served as a royal residence for centuries. In fact, the Palace of the Normans, also known as the Palazzo Orleans, was the first home of King Louis Philippe and of his Neapolitan wife Maria Amelia. Inherited by her descendants, the palace was owned by the Orleans until the XX century.

Roger II's successors were not as lucky. The kingdom suffered various invasions and foreign occupations and by 1198 the House of Hauteville was no more. In fact, already in 1194 Holy Roman Emperor Henry VI, who had married a daughter of King Roger II, invaded the Kingdom of Sicily and caused great upheaval, eventually claiming the throne for himself. The Hohenstaufens, as Henry VI's dynasty was known, remained rulers of Sicily until 1266 when Prince Charles of Anjou, a son of King Louis VIII of France overthrew King Manfred.

Further political upheaval continued when the Sicilian rose in revolt against Charles I and forced him to relocate to Naples, where he established a new capital. In Sicily, however, power rested on King Peter III of Aragon, Charles I's son-in-law, considered one of the greatest medieval monarchs. After him, the House of Aragon remained in control of Sicily until the XV century when King Martin II died childless in 1410 and his realm was incorporated into the Aragonese monarchy.

King Ferdinand the Catholic inherited the Sicilian crown in 1468. He was consumed with constant warfare in Italy, particularly after King Charles VIII of France invaded Naples and overthrew King Alfonso II, a cousin of Ferdinand's. After decades of warfare, the French were defeated and Naples and Sicily were placed under the rule of Spanish monarch, who in 1519 became Emperor Charles V. His descendants were to rule for the next two centuries.

In 1713, the Spanish crown lost Naples and Sicily after signing the Treaty of Utrecht, which redesigned the map of Europe and allowed the Bourbons to remain rulers in Spain. Louis XIV, who had married the Spanish Infanta María Teresa, orchestrated the succession of their grandson, Philippe d'Anjou, as King of Spain since María Teresa's half-brother, Carlos II, died childless in 1700. This astute political move, however, plunged Europe into a lengthy conflict since the other major powers feared that France gaining Spain would completely destroy the continent's balance of power. When peace finally arrived in 1713, Felipe V of Spain (Philippe d'Anjou) had to relinquish his Italian possessions to the Duke of Savoy, who ruled briefly until losing the kingdom to the Austrians in 1720 as part of a new peace treaty signed in The Hague.

The Royal Palace of Caserta.

Fifteen years later, Duke Carlo of Parma and Piacenza, the eldest son of King Felipe V and of his Parmesan wife, Isabella Farnese, invaded Naples and conquered the kingdom. Austria being far more interested in gaining territory in Poland eventually ceded the Southern Italian possessions to Duke of Parma, who as King of Naples and Sicily ruled with the name of King Carlo VII of Naples and V of Sicily.

King Carlo was one of the best examples of enlightened despotism to ever sit on a throne. He was described as, *"probably the most successful European ruler of his generation. He had provided firm, consistent, intelligent leadership. He had chosen capable ministers.... [his] personal life had won the respect of the people."* As such, he joined a distinguished small number of monarchs who included King Friedrich II of Prussia and Empress Maria Theresa. Their choice of governing style was inspired by the Enlightenment. These monarchs embraced its emphasis on rationality and *"tended to allow religious toleration, freedom of speech and the press, and the right to hold private property. Most fostered the arts, sciences, and education."* King Carlo's architectural and artistic legacy is present to this day all around the former kingdom and includes jewels such as the royal palaces of Caserta, Naples, Portici and Capodimonte, to name but the best known.

In 1738 King Carlo married Princess Maria Amalia, daughter of King Augustus III of Poland and of his Habsburg wife, the former Archduchess Maria Josepha of Austria, daughter of Emperor Joseph I, an uncle of Empress Maria Theresa. Carlo and Maria Amalia were the parents of a large family of thirteen children born between 1740-1757: Maria Isabel (1740-1742); Maria Josefa (b/d 1742); Maria Isabel (1743-1749); Maria Josefa (1744-1801); Maria Luisa (1745-1792), wife of Emperor Leopold II; Filippo, Duke of Calabria (1747-1777); Carlos IV of Spain (1748-1819), married to Princess Maria Luisa of Parma, a niece of King Carlo; Maria Teresa (1749-1750); Ferdinando I of the Two Sicilies (1751-1825); Gabriel (1752-1788), who married Infanta Mariana Vitoria of Portugal; Antonio (1755-1817), who married his niece Infanta Maria Amalia of Spain; and Francesco (1757-1771). All these children were born in Southern Italy. When their father succeeded as King Carlos III of Spain they accompanied the royal couple on their journey to Madrid, with the exception of the Duke of Calabria and King Ferdinando I who remained in Naples and ruled until his death in 1825.

As monarch, Ferdinando I left the every-day running of his realm to his ministers. The enlightenment that his father had brought to Naples was quickly abandoned and conservative and Church forces at court quickly gained the upper hand. These factions were shocked by news of events in Paris in 1789. The revolution's blood thirst not only led to the execution of King Louis XVI and Queen

Marie Antoinette four years later, but it gained France the enmity of King Ferdinando and Queen Maria Carolina, who never forgave the French for killing her sister. Hence, in 1798 King Ferdinando I began a long and costly war to eradicate French influence in Italian affairs. That year he struck and conquered Rome, a pyric victory of short duration but lasting effect. The following year the French invaded the Neapolitan kingdom with considerable detriment to King Ferdinando.

Unhappy with Napoleon's victories across Europe, Ferdinando, encouraged by his wife, joined the Third Coalition against the French Emperor. Within a year, however, the Third Coalition was defeated and most of Europe lay at Napoleon's feet. The French emperor lost little time in taking Naples and installing his brother-in-law Joachim Murat as "King of the Two Sicilies." Ferdinando I and Maria Carolina, who fled Naples before the French arrived, established their own court in Palermo, where they were to remain for nearly a decade.

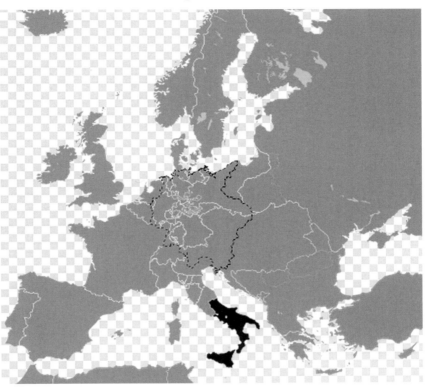

Area in black represents the geographical location of the Kingdom of the Two Sicilies.

The Kingdom of the Two Sicilies lasted from 1816 until 1860, when Garibaldi invaded and dethroned King Francesco II. The realm was annexed into the Kingdom of Sardinia under King Vittorio Emanuele II of Savoy, who in 1861 became the first modern-era monarch of the Kingdom of Italy.

Francesco II, after a valiant last stand at Gaeta, was forced into exile. He initially settled in Rome under the protection of Pope Pius IX. The royal family lived in reduced circumstances in the Farnese Palace, which they had inherited from the Dukes of Parma along with many other properties. These possessions, in fact, where the only source of revenue left to the family since the Savoys never paid the Bourbons of the Two Sicilies any compensation for the loss of their vast properties and priceless art collections.

A large number of Neapolitans and Sicilians remained loyal to the Bourbon Dynasty. Many of these supporters feared that under the rule of the Northern Italian Savoys Southern Italy would suffer economic dislocation. As it turned out, the Savoy rule was a disappointment and the once proud and prosperous Kingdom of the Two Sicilies witnessed, *"Abject poverty ... and thousands decided to leave in search of a better future."* This diaspora was the main reason behind the large migration of Southern Italians to countries that welcomed immigrants such as the United States, Argentina and Australia.

After Napoleon's defeat in 1814, Joachim reached an agreement with Austria and was allowed to retain the throne of Naples. Ferdinando's diplomats were unsuccessful in securing their king his old kingdom. Murat's decision to support Napoleon's return in 1815 sealed his fate when he sided with his brother-in-law. The Austrians moved against Murat, defeated him and restored Ferdinando in Naples. Unwilling to accept his defeat, Murat attempted a comeback but was defeated, captured and executed. The following year both kingdoms, Naples and Sicily, were formally united as a new political entity and King Ferdinando IV of Naples finally became King Ferdinando I of the Two Sicilies.

Today, members of the Bourbon dynasty visit their former kingdom with some frequency. Each visit raises considerable interest among the population, who now think of Bourbon rule as one of the most prosperous periods of their once proud kingdom, Europe's strongest realm south of Rome.

3

CHAPTER I

Ferdinando I "Nasone"

Ferdinando was only eight years old when he succeeded to the throne. His father had become King of Spain in 1759 on the death of his half-brother King Ferdinand VI, and resigned the throne of Naples and Sicily, which had come to him by the Treaty of Vienna in 1735, to the young Ferdinand, who was IV of Naples and III of Sicily. As he was a minor, a Council of Regency was formed to rule for him, headed by one Bernardo Tanucci. Tanucci paid little attention to the young King's development and neglected his education altogether, with the result that Ferdinando grew up lacking all social graces and barely literate. His favored pastimes were shooting and fishing and his favored companions were palace servants and stable boys. King Ferdinando could not be more disinterested in conducting the affairs of state that came with wearing a crown. His personal appearance was also not attractive – he had a rather long nose that quickly gained him the nickname "Nasone." Despite these drawbacks he was good-natured and easy-going and was popular with the ordinary people.

Ferdinando was declared of age in January 1767. Immediately, Neapolitan diplomats began searching Europe for a consort for their young king. Their choice settled on Archduchess Maria Josepha, one of Empress Maria Theresa's many daughters, who included luckless Queen Marie Antoinette of France.

Opposite page: an imposing portrait of King Ferdinando I surrounded by all the trappings of his high office.

Above: a younger portrait of King Ferdinando I, who was born in Naples on January 18, 1751.

Left: King Ferdinando I and Queen Maria Carolina in 1782. Surrounding them are six of their children.

A young King Ferdinando I of Naples, at about the time when a wife was being sought for him.

Archduchess Maria Carolina of Austria was not first expected to marry the King of Naples, but she had to after her sister's death.

Unfortunately, Maria Josepha died just before departing to Naples, leaving Ferdinando I to consider one of her sisters as a possible replacement. The burden then fell on Archduchess Maria Carolina (1752-1814), an indomitable woman who was willful and impetuous, while also believing herself better prepared to rule than her weakling of a husband. In fact, in the negotiations surrounding her marriage, Maria Carolina was given the right to sit in the state council as soon as she gave birth to an heir.

Maria Carolina was much more intelligent and cultured than her loutish husband and supplied the necessary graces at court. She was, in countless ways, the real power behind the throne. As soon as she could, Maria Carolina began playing an active role in affairs of state, all the while gaining great ascendancy on her weak-willed husband. The French Revolution horrified Maria Carolina. She never forgave the French for the horrific end handed to her sister and her husband and children. Consequently, Maria Carolina became a sworn enemy of Revolutionary France, supporting every single coalition organized to turn back the clock.

Despite their differences the marriage was happy and

Archduchess Maria Josepha of Austria, Ferdinando I's first fiancée.

Maria Carolina produced no less than eighteen children, who would connect the Sicilian Royal Family to many of Europe's Catholic thrones: Maria Theresa (1772-1807), wife of Emperor Franz II, her first cousin; Luisa (1773-1802), married to Grand Duke Ferdinando III of Tuscany, her first cousin; Carlo (1775-1778); Anna (1775-1780); Francesco I; Maria (1779-1783); Cristina (1779-1849), married to King Carlo-Felice of Sardinia; Gennaro (1780-1789); Giuseppe (1781-1783); Maria-Amelia (1782-1866), married to King Louis Philippe of the French; stillborn daughter in 1783; Antonietta (1784-1806), who married her first cousin future King Fernando VII of Spain; Clotilde (1786-1792); Enricheta (1787-1792); Carlo (1788-1789(; Leopold (1790-1851), married to Archduchess Clementine of Austria (1816-1881); Alberto (1792-1798); and Isabella (1793-1801).

In 1798 Napoleon's troops invaded Italy, and it was the British Admiral Horatio Nelson who conducted the Royal Family from Naples to safety in Sicily. After two years they were able to return to Naples, but were driven out again in 1806.

King Ferdinando I and Queen Maria Carolina of Naples, she was the power behind the throne.

Napoleon appointed his brother Joseph as King of Naples before replacing him with Prince Joachim Murat. Joachim's zone of control was restricted to the mainland region of the Kingdom of Naples, Ferdinando remaining on Sicily. As for Joseph Bonaparte, he was sent to Spain to sit on the throne that Napoleon had gained in 1808 when he organized the overthrow and imprisonment of King Carlos IV and the royal family.

Ferdinando I and Maria Carolina, accompanied by their children, settled comfortably in Sicily, from where she continued conspiring against the French. In due time, she forgave her cousin the Duke d'Orléans and allowed Louis Philippe to marry her daughter Maria-Amelia (Marie-Amelie). Through this marriage, more than any other, Maria Carolina's blood permeated most of Europe's Catholic courts.

As the tide turned against Napoleon, Maria Carolina was delirious with joy. She had nearly gone mad with rage when Napoleon defeated the Austrians in 1809 and made it all the way to Vienna. Her rage reached even higher bounds when in 1810 her former son-in-law (and nephew) Emperor Franz allowed Napoleon to marry his daughter, Archduchess Marie Louise. Through this marriage, Queen Maria Carolina became the great-grandmother of the King of Rome, the only son fathered by Napoleon with his Austrian wife.

The throne room inside the Royal Palace in Naples.

Queen Maria Carolina never forgave the French for the fate they handed her sister Marie Antoinette. In this portrait we see the tragic French queen with her children.

The Bonapartist adventure in Southern Italy finally came tumbling down after Napoleon's loss at the Battle of Waterloo in 1815. King Joachim lost both the throne and his life, and Naples was restored to King Ferdinando, who in terms of the Congress of Vienna assumed the title of King Ferdinando I of the Two Sicilies. To reduce mounting civil unrest, in 1821 he was persuaded to grant a Constitution to the country.

In April 1814, Maria Carolina received delightful news: the complete defeat of the French. The Allies vanquished Napoleon and the French Empire was at an end since his abdication and the naming of Marie Louise as regent was rejected. Sadly, Maria Carolina did not have long to savor this victory.

Queen Maria Carolina had sought refuge in Austria, where her nephew the Emperor was most unappreciative of her efforts to meddle in politics. She looked forward to the upcoming gathering of diplomats to exert major benefits for her kingdom. However, as the Congress of Vienna convened, Queen Maria Carolina's days came to an end. She died of apoplexy on September 8, 1814. With indecent haste Ferdinando married his long-term mistress Donna Lucia Migliaccio, Duchess of Floridia. He spent the remainder of his reign quietly, indulging in his favorite pastime of hunting, and died in 1825.

Above left: Grand Duchess Luisa of Tuscany, consort of Grand Duke Ferdinando III.

Above right: Empress Maria Theresa of Austria, consort of Holy Roman Emperor Franz II, later Emperor Franz I of Austria.

Right: Queen Marie Amélie, consort of King Louis Philippe of the French.

Interestingly, through their descendants, Ferdinando I and Maria Carolina were the great-grandparents of a truly unique group of people: The King of Rome, Emperor Pedro II of Brazil, Queen Maria II of Portugal, Grand Duke Ferdinando IV of Tuscany, King Ludwig III of Bavaria, King Vittorio Emanuel II of Italy, the Count of Paris and his brother the Duke of Chartres, King Leopold II of the Belgians, Empress Carlota of Mexico, Duke Philipp of Württemberg, the Count d'Eu (consort of the Princess Imperial Isabel of Brazil), King Ferdinand of Bulgaria, Queen Mercedes of Spain, the Countess of Paris and her brother the Duke of Galliera, the Count de Chambord, Duchess Louise of Parma, King Consort Francisco de Asís of Spain and his wife Queen Isabel II, King Francesco II of the Two Sicilies, the Count of Caserta and his wife Antonietta, and Duchess Maria Pia of Parma, first wife of Duke Roberto I.

This is an impressive list of descendants, particularly when we look at the names found in the following generations. While most genealogical studies have paid great attention to Queen Victoria and her list of descendants, an impressive number of people, these are dwarfed by the number of European royals descended from Ferdinando I and Maria Carolina of the Two Sicilies.

CHAPTER II
Francesco I

Born in Naples in 1777, Francesco was Ferdinando's second but eldest surviving son, and was 47 years old when he came to the Throne.

In 1797 he married his double first cousin Archduchess Maria Clementina of Austria, third daughter of the Holy Roman Emperor Leopold II, and by her had a son and a daughter. While the couple's son died a few months after his birth, their daughter grew up to have an interesting life. Her name was Maria Carolina and in 1816 she married Prince Charles of France, Duke de Berry, who was assassinated four years later. At the time of her husband's death, Maria Carolina was pregnant with their second child, their first child being a girl, Louise Marie, destined to marry into the Parmesan branch of the Bourbon dynasty. Nearly six months after her husband's death, Maria Carolina gave birth to a son, Henri, Count de Chambord, the last of the mainline Bourbons. In fact, had his uncle the Duke of Orléans not accepted the throne in 1830, Henri would have succeeded his grandfather King Charles X. Maria Amelia, as consort of King Louis Philippe remained deeply respectful of the legitimacy represented by her grandnephew.

The marriage of Francesco and Maria Clementina was happy. However, her weak constitution was always a source of much concern. Unfortunately, Maria Clementina developed tuberculosis and died in 1801.

Opposite page: an official portrait of King Francesco I in military uniform and decorations, the Golden Fleece prominently displayed around his neck.

Above: a younger portrait of King Francesco I, who was born in Naples on August 19, 1777.

Left: King Francesco I, Queen Maria Isabel and their children paying homage to his father, the late King Ferdinando I.

The following year Francesco remarried as the throne had to be provided with an heir in the next generation. His second wife was the Infanta Maria Isabel, fifth daughter of King Carlos IV of Spain by his Italian wife Princess

The Duchess de Berry, née Princess Maria Carolina Ferdinanda of Naples.

Maria Luisa of Bourbon-Parma. As was the case with his first wife, Maria Isabel was also Francesco's first cousin. By her he had a large family of six sons and six daughters: Luisa Carlotta (1804-1844), who married her first cousin the Infante Francisco de Paula of Spain (by whom she became the mother of King Francisco de Asís, husband of Queen Isabel II of Spain); Maria Cristina (1806-1878), the fourth wife of her Uncle Fernando VII of Spain (by whom she became the mother of Queen Isabel II); Ferdinando II; Carlo Ferdinando (1811-1862), Prince of Capua, who married morganatically a lady by the name of Penelope Smyth (1815-1882); Leopold (1813-1860), who married Princess Maria Vittoria of Savoy (1814-1874); Maria Antonietta (1814-1898), who married Grand Duke Leopoldo II of Tuscany (1797-1870); Antonio (1816-1843), Count of Lecce; Maria Amelia (1818-1857), who married Infante Sebastián of Spain (1811-1875); Maria Carolina (1820-1861); who married her first cousin Infante Carlos of Spain (1818-1861); Teresa Cristina (1822-1889), who married Emperor Pedro II of Brazil (1825-1891); Luigi (1824-1897), Count of Aquila, who married Princess Januaria of Brazil (1822-1901); and Francesco di Paola (1827-1892), Count of Trapani, who married Archduchess Isabella of Austria-Tuscany (1834-1901).

The Napoleonic invasion forced the Sicilian departure from Naples to Palermo in 1806. Desperate times called for desperate measures and Lord William Bentinck, Great Britain's leading diplomatic representative in the Two Sicilies, also played an important political role in the effort to pass a constitution that stripped King Ferdinando I of all power. Six years later, the King's eldest surviving son, Francesco, who was considered a liberal, was appointed regent with British support.

This brief liberal constitutional period came to an end when Napoleon fell and Ferdinando I returned to Naples. The constitution was suppressed and both kingdoms, Naples and Sicily, were incorporated into a new realm, that of the Two Sicilies (1816). Francesco then assumed the revived title of Duke of Calabria, as heir to his father's throne. While still heir apparent he professed liberal ideas, and on the outbreak of the revolution of 1820 he

Opposite page: Archduchess Maria Clementina of Austria, first wife of future King Francesco I of the Two Sicilies. Through her daughter, Maria Carolina, King Francesco I was the grandfather of the both the Count de Chambord and the Duchess of Parma, who in turn was the grandmother of Empress Zita of Austria, Queen of Hungary.

accepted the regency apparently in a friendly spirit toward the new constitution.

Infanta Luisa Carlota of Spain, born princess of Naples, mother of King Francisco de Asís of Spain.

Francesco's dabbling with liberalism, however, ended upon his succession to the throne in 1825, when he pursued a conservative course. He took little part in the government, which he left in the hands of favorites and police officials, and lived with his mistresses, surrounded by soldiers, ever in dread of assassination. During his reign the only revolutionary movement was the outbreak on the Cilento (1828), repressed by the Marquis Delcarretto, an ex-liberal. He was, however, successful in having the Austrian occupation force withdrawn (1827) therefore relieving a large financial burden on the treasury.

Long overshadowed by his father, Francesco made little mark on the political scene. All in all, his reign was fairly uneventful and he died in Naples in November 1830. Francesco I was buried in the royal crypt inside the Basilica of Santa Chiara in Naples.

Queen Maria Isabel, who was described as *"good natured and pliable,"* spent most of her time focused on charitable work. She had no interest in politics, unlike her indomitable mother-in-law. She was well matched with her husband and their happy marriage, in spite of his countless infidelities, was rather fruitful. Perhaps it was both her dislike of politics and lack of political acumen that earned her the love of her husband's subjects. She was extremely polite and well mannered and her generosity knew no bounds. All her children were very deferential to Maria Isabel, particularly the Prince of Capua, on whose behalf she tried to intervene with her son the King when he forbade Capua to marry morganatically. Ferdinando II was furious with his brother, who eloped with Ms. Smyth and married her in Scotland in 1836. Consequently, most of Capua's estates were confiscated and his allowance rescinded.

Queen Maria Isabel of the Two Sicilies.

Ferdinando II never again set eyes on his brother, who was forced to live in exile. Capua and his wife had two children, a son and a daughter. A life of indebtedness and uncertainty took its toll on Capua. In the 1850s a contemporary wrote, *"The Prince is stout, vulgar, and usually rigged up like a rustic charlatan. He is adorned with a long and dirty grey beard, and his hair is also long, dirty and grey."*

In 1859 Capua's fortunes seemed to improve when his nephew Francesco II ordered the restoration of both a pension and the prince's estates. However, that was lost the following year when the Kingdom of the Two Sicilies ceased to exist. Capua died poor and forgotten in 1862. His widow and children lived near Lucca in the beautiful Castello di Marlia, a property owned by the Bourbons of Parma. Penelope, who used the title of Countess of Mascali, after an estate owned by her husband, died there in 1882. Neither of their children married and left descendants.

Queen Maria Isabel was spared seeing her beloved Capua fall into such a state of disgrace. She died at the Palace of Portici in September 1848. She was laid to rest at the Basilica of Santa Chiara.

King Francesco I of the Two Sicilies.

Above: An official portrait of good-natured, and fun-loving, Queen Maria Isabel of the Two Sicilies.

Left: Prince Carlo Ferdinando (1811-1862), Prince of Capua.

Below: A scene from within the royal palace depicting the children of King Francesco I playing various musical instruments.

King Francesco, prematurely aged, died in 1830.

Interestingly, Queen Maria Isabel is said to have inherited her mother's predilection for amorous escapades. Acton describes this tendency as, *"a weakness for men, preferably robust and younger than herself, irrespective of class."* A widow at the age of forty, the Dowager Queen sought companionship in the embrace of various men at court, one of them an Austrian officer, Baron von Schmuckher, whose peccadilloes with Maria Isabel cost him her son expelling the Austrian from the kingdom. In 1839, the Papal Nuncio informed the Vatican that the lonesome Dowager Queen had finally found companionship in the embrace of Count Francesco del Balzo, a brother of the prominent Duke of Presenzano. The groom was sixteen years the bride's junior. The King, her son, is said to not only have approved of his mother's decision, but also to have attended the secret wedding ceremony. Del Balzo's position at court did not change after his marriage, treated basically as a morganatic union, as *"the husband takes no rank of consequence,"* in spite of the union. Nine years their union lasted, and as

Queen María Luisa of Spain, mother-in-law of King Francesco I.

King Carlos IV of Spain, father-in-law of King Francesco I.

Prince Carlo Ferdinando, Prince of Capua.

The Countess of Mascali, née Penelope Smyth.

Queen Regent Maria Cristina of Spain.

Emperor Pedro II and Empress Teresa Cristina of Brazil.

Princess Maria Vittoria, Countess of Siracusa.

expected, and quite likely to everyone's relief, the couple had no offspring. Del Balzo survived his queenly wife by more than three decades, dying in 1882.

While King Francesco I and Queen Maria Isabel's daughters found destinies abroad, where they were married into some of the continent's main royal Catholic families, the royal couple's younger sons had a more difficult time finding place and purpose in life. We have already visited the difficult life of the Prince of Capua, Carlo Ferdinando, who spent decades in exile because of his desire to avoid duty and obligations to follow the dictates of his heart. The four youngest sons of Francesco I (Siracusa, Lecce, Aquila and Trapani) and his second wife, had an equally difficult time finding purpose, even though at least in the matrimonial stakes, they all fulfilled what was expected, even if unhappily so.

Leopoldo, Count of Siracusa, served as Lieutenant General of Sicily under

Prince Leopold, Count of Siracusa.

the appointment of his brother King Ferdinando II. Siracusa lived in Palermo and while serving there, he introduced important social and political reforms, much in need to modernize the Sicilian half of the kingdom. One historian best described Siracusa's political ideas when describing him as making, *"no bones about his liberal opinions."* This decision made Siracusa very popular, which in turn sealed his fate in Naples, where the King recalled Siracusa in 1835.

When it came to finding Siracusa a bride, the situation proved equally cumbersome. King Ferdinand II wanted his brother to marry Princess Marie d'Orléans, second daughter of King Louis Philippe and of his Sicilian wife, Marie Amélie, a sister of King Francesco I, Siracusa's late father. However, the negotiations failed when the French monarch refused to grant the dowry requested by Siracusa's brother.

King Louis Philippe of the French.

Instead, Prince Leopoldo was married off to Princess Maria Vittoria of Savoy, second daughter of the Count of Villafranca. The couple turned out to be ill suited, and even though a daughter was born to them (the child lived one day), they soon parted ways. Leopoldo was a bon vivant and an artist, who was more at ease leading a life of leisure, while dedicated to his artistic interests.

Between 1846-1850, Siracusa lived abroad. When revolution threatened the thrones of Europe in 1848, he let his opinion be known when claiming that a Constitution *"would save the whole family from the ruin that threatens us."* In spite of it all, Siracusa was King Ferdinando II's favorite brother and he would settle his brother's debts on more then one occasion. Harold Acton, in his opus on the Bourbons of the Two Sicilies, described Siracusa as, *"a large, powerful man, with a very handsome countenance."* Unfortunately, Siracusa's fast living took a toll on his body and in 1854 he suffered a debilitating stroke. Although he recovered, his hedonistic days were counted.

Prince Antonio, Count of Lecce.

Princess Louise Marie of France (Duchess of Parma).

Carlo III, Duke of Parma.

The Count of Siracusa was among those at court who wished his nephew, Francesco II, would form a close alliance with Savoy against the Vatican. Not doing so, Siracusa believed, would bring certain doom to Naples. He also urged the King to make liberal concessions to stem the tied of revolution unleashed by Garibaldi and the Thousand, but all his counsel went unheeded. With the kingdom collapsing all around, Siracusa left and settled in Piedmont. He died in Pisa in December 1860, a few weeks short of the end of the siege of Gaeta. His estranged wife, who had retired to a convent, an atmosphere better suited to her ultramontane opinions, died in Naples in 1874.

Prince Antonio, Count of Lecce, had an affinity for the pleasures of the flesh, much like his elder brothers. In spite of suffering from ill health and general physical weakness, the young man was considered quite successful in amorous matters. Hence, finding him a settlement became a matter of great importance. King Ferdinando II wished Lecce to marry their niece Princess Louise Marie of France, the eldest child of the troublesome Duchess de Berry, Maria

Prince Luigi, Count of Aquila.

Princess Januaria, Countess of Aquila.

Carolina. Louise Marie stood to inherit a large fortune and the Sicilian monarch wanted to secure his brother Lecce's future. Unfortunately for Lecce, the princess escaped his hands and she was married instead to the future Duke Carlo III of Parma. Lecce's life after the failure of this matrimonial scheme was consumed by his worsening health. Consumed *"by a precarious state of health, having had repeated attacks of paralysis,"* Lecce fell to typhoid fever in January 1843.

Prince Luigi, Count of Aquila, was destined from an early age to serve in the Neapolitan royal navy. In the early 1840s, Aquila was offered as a possible husband to nubile Queen Isabel II of Spain. The plan did not succeed and instead Aquila sailed to Brazil as a member of the entourage

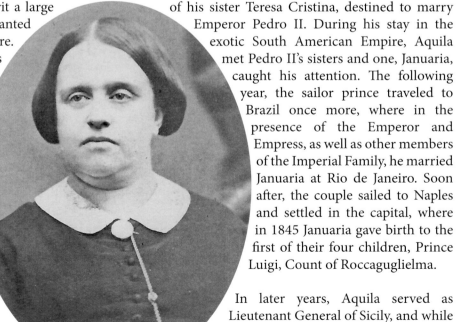

Princess Januaria, Countess of Aquila.

of his sister Teresa Cristina, destined to marry Emperor Pedro II. During his stay in the exotic South American Empire, Aquila met Pedro II's sisters and one, Januaria, caught his attention. The following year, the sailor prince traveled to Brazil once more, where in the presence of the Emperor and Empress, as well as other members of the Imperial Family, he married Januaria at Rio de Janeiro. Soon after, the couple sailed to Naples and settled in the capital, where in 1845 Januaria gave birth to the first of their four children, Prince Luigi, Count of Roccaguglielma.

In later years, Aquila served as Lieutenant General of Sicily, and while there demonstrated his predilection for liberalism and reform. His political views, however, were later used against Aquila by the ultra-Conservative

The Countess of Aquila with her children, from left: Prince Filippo, Princess Maria Isabella and Prince Luigi, Count of Roccaguglielma.

Prince Francesco di Paola, Count of Trapani.

camarilla surrounding King Francesco II. At a time when Francesco II needed good direction, Aquila and Siracusa were ignored because they recommended reform, the adoption of a constitution and an alliance with Piedmont against the Pope. Nothing Aquila advised was paid any attention to since his enemies at court convinced the King that the prince his uncle was looking after his own interests and not those of the dynasty. Hence, with the kingdom collapsing all around him, the Count of Aquila departed Naples in August 1860. In due time he settled in France, where he died in 1897. His wife, Princess Januaria survived him by four years, dying in Nice in 1901.

Of the Aquila children, only two of the sons (Luigi, Count of Roccaguglielma and Filippo) lived to reach adulthood. Both princes married morganatically, but only Luigi left descendants from his marriage to a Ms. Amelia Bellow-Hamel.

Prince Francesco di Paola, Count of Trapani, was but three years of age at the time of his father's death in 1830. In his teens, the prince was sent to study at the Jesuit College in Rome, as he was expected to enter the Church. Lacking vocation, Trapani changed course when his name was suggested as one of the candidates for the hand of his cousin, and niece, Queen Isabel II of Spain. This scheme was unsuccessful and instead

Trapani married Archduchess Maria Isabella of Austria-Tuscany, his niece, in 1850.

Archduchess Maria Isabella, Countess of Trapani.

The following year they became the parents of a daughter, Maria Antonietta, who in 1868 married her first cousin Prince Alfonso, Count of Caserta. Five other children joined the family, but only another daughter, Maria Carolina, reached adulthood. She married in 1885 Polish Count Andrzej Zamoyski and two of her eight children were destined to marry back into the Sicilian family. Princess Maria Carolina spent most of her life in Poland and she died in Warsaw in 1941 during the Nazi occupation.

Politically, Trapani belonged to the camarilla that advised King Francesco II to take a hardline against the Piedmontese and in support of the Vatican. Queen Maria Theresa, widow of Trapani's brother Ferdinando II, found in Trapani a reliable, conservative ally, even if lacking in the intellectual capabilities required to succeed her as leader of the camarilla after her death in 1867. In time, Trapani settled in France, as was the case with many of his relations. He died in Paris in 1892. His widow survived him until 1901 when she died in Bürgenstock, near Lucerne, Switzerland.

The Trapani children, from left: Maria Carolina, Maria Antonietta, Maria Annunziata and Leopoldo.

CHAPTER III

Ferdinando II
"King Bomba"

History has not been kind to King Ferdinando II, whose undeserved reputation in most of Europe can be compared to that of the worst Italian brigand. Vilified and lampooned in sections of the liberal press he is best known by his nickname "King Bomba."

Succeeding his father Francesco as King in 1830 at the age of only 20, Ferdinando was at first a popular monarch, whose easy going manners endeared him to all sections of the population, and who was active, hardworking and conscientious. The *"lazzaroni,"* the lower classes of Neapolitan society were quite fond of the King. On his accession he issued a proclamation stating that his goal was to govern his Kingdom in a way that would bring the greatest happiness to the greatest number of his subjects, and in the early years of his reign he affected many changes for the better in the country. These included a reduction in taxation and a cut in expenditures, all in a concerted effort to cleanse the public coffers. He had the first railway

King Ferdinando II.

in Italy built (between Naples and the Palace of Portici) and established telegraphic communications between Naples and Palermo.

He was, however, narrow-minded and obstinate and a partisan of an authoritarian form of government, convinced of an almost divine right to rule, heavily under the influence of the Church, violently opposed to the on growing movement toward Italian unification, and would brook no opposition to his rule. In 1837 he suppressed a Sicilian demand for a new constitution and governed with the aid of a vigilant secret police force. Liberal agitators rapidly found themselves in jail and there was heavy press censorship. Ten years later riots in Reggio, Calabria and Messina were put down by the military, and in 1848 there was an uprising on the island of Sicily, which had as its aim the secession of the island from the rest of the Kingdom, and whose leaders declared the King deposed. His response was to raise an army of 20,000 men and set forth to subdue the island.

His navy bombarded the town of Messina with the utmost severity and hundreds of civilians died in the destruction. It was this action, which caused the nickname of "King Bomba" to be attached to him, and led to the opprobrium of the press throughout Europe. The future British Prime Minister William Gladstone described Ferdinando as *"the negation of God."* The King himself was totally impervious to this criticism from abroad and convinced of his absolute right to rule.

During the year of revolution, 1848, Ferdinando II came to the aid of Pope Pius IX and granted him asylum at Gaeta. Once the uprisings in Rome were put down, the Pope returned to his capital and he never forgot Ferdinando II's hospitality.

In his private life, however, Ferdinando was exemplary. In 1832 he married Princess Maria Cristina of Savoy, daughter of King Vittorio Emanuele I of Sardinia, a pious young lady of sterling qualities who was much loved and much mourned when she died in childbirth at the age of 23, after giving birth to a son and heir,

Queen Maria Christina of the Two Sicilies.

Crown Prince Francesco. One year later Ferdinando remarried — his second wife Archduchess Maria Theresa of Austria belonged to the immensely wealthy Teschen branch of the House of Habsburg. She gave him no less than 12 children and the King proved a devoted husband and father, with no hint of scandal attached to his private life. The family moved between the Royal Palace in Naples and the other family properties, notably the magnificent Reggio di Caserta, the Italian equivalent of Versailles. Their private family life was extremely frugal, one nineteenth century chronicler, Countess Bernstorff, describes meeting the family in the 1850s *"...the room they were in was very spacious but sparsely furnished...the Queen sat down on one of the little chairs...she often sits here for hours at a time, busy with her crochet...the domestic life of the King and Queen is the most beautiful thing imaginable. They are a most united couple and tenderly devoted to their children, whom they always have with them...."* Another report from the time says, *"The family lived with the greatest parsimony, living for most of the time on macaroni."*

Queen Maria Theresa was primarily concerned with her husband and large band of children and had little time for social obligations. Highly religious, she was under the influence of Jesuit priests and made few public appearances. Both she and the King

King Ferdinando II in earlier years.

A portrait of King Ferdinando II of the Two Sicilies.

were criticized by certain sections for this dereliction to duty but paid little attention.

King Francesco II, only son of King Ferdinando II and Queen Maria Christina.

As mentioned previously, Ferdinando II and Maria Theresa were a prolific couple. Between 1838 and 1857, the Queen gave birth to a dozen offspring: Lodovico (Luigi) (1838-1886), Count of Trani, who married Mathilde Duchess in Bavaria (1849-1925), one of the sisters of Empress Elisabeth of Austria; Alberto (1839-1844), Count of Castrogiovanni; Alfonso, Count of Caserta; Maria Annunziata (1843-1871), who married Archduke Karl Ludwig of Austria and was thus the mother of Archduke Franz Ferdinand, as well as the great-grandmother of Emperor Karl I; Maria Immacolata (1844-1899), who married Archduke Karl Salvator of Austria-Tuscany(1839-1892); Gaetano (1846-1871), Count of Girgenti, who married Infanta Isabel of Spain, eldest daughter of Queen Isabel II; Giuseppe (1848-1851), Count of Lucera; Maria Pia (1849-1882), first wife of Duke Roberto I of Parma (1848-1907); Vincenzo, Count of Milazzo (1851-1854); Pasquale (1852-1905), Count of Bari, who married Blanche de Marconnay (1848-1926); Maria Luisa (1855-1874), who married Prince Enrico of Bourbon-Parma (1851-1905), Count of Bardi; and Gennaro (1857-1867), Count of Caltagirone.

In 1856 King Ferdinando survived an assassination attempt. Many believe that the monarch never truly recovered from the bayonet wound he received, this leading to his untimely end. He fell gravely ill just as Sardinia and France declared war on Austria, a campaign that led to Giuseppe Garibaldi's invasion with the "Mille," the thousand mercenary soldiers who sailed with him and landed in the island of Sicily. Ferdinando II did not live long enough to see the success of the Risorgimento. After long suffering, he died at Caserta in May 1859, thus being spared the loss of his kingdom a year later.

Maria Theresa, contrary to popular belief, was very fond of her stepson Francesco II. He in turn was very respectful of his stepmother, who at times called him *"her son,"* even though

Queen María Teresa, second wife of King Ferdinando II.

she neglected his education and spared no effort to advance the station of her own sons. Although she had a retiring nature, Maria Theresa did not shy away from expressing her political opinion, particularly to her husband and stepson. A Habsburg to her very core, the Queen had little time for liberals and constitutions. She advised strong-arm tactics and asked her husband to be strict as a monarch.

Widowhood, never an easy time, was particularly difficult for Queen Maria Theresa. She intended to remain a close confidant of Francesco II, whom she wanted to continue the authoritarian policies espoused by her late husband. This decision, however, only led to the further erosion of the King's support among his discontented subjects. Maria Theresa did not enjoy a close relationship with her stepson's wife, Maria Sophia Duchess in Bavaria, who tried her best to secure the reduction of her stepmother-in-law's influence.

In 1860, when Garibaldi and the Savoy defeated the Kingdom of the Two Sicilies, Maria Theresa found refuge in Rome, where the Pope welcomed the Sicilians with open arms. There she lived in a rented palace, although the family later moved into the Farnese Palace, a large structure the Neapolitans had inherited from their Parmesan ancestors.

Queen Maria Theresa of the Two Sicilies.

The Royal Family of the Two Sicilies. At center is Queen Maria Theresa, surrounded by her younger children. To the right are Queen Maria Sophia and her sister Princess Mathilde. At left, with his brothers, is King Francesco II.

For several years, Maria Theresa and her children lived in Rome, not traveling much. Then tragedy struck again The latest misery that befell the Sicilians began with the Queen's death in Albano on August 5, 1867. Ten year-old Prince Gennaro followed his mother to an early grave two days later.

Behind, Queen Maria Theresa left a large brood of children and youngsters living in exile. Luckily, for the orphaned Sicilians, their relations at the Austrian Imperial Court assured that, at the very least, the princesses would find acceptable husbands in Vienna. The Sicilians, recipients of the largesse of wealthier relations, were raised by reputable instructors and received well-rounded education. The princesses were taught the arts and music, while also learning various languages. The princes were eventually found commissions in various royal armies. They all had productive and somewhat prominent lives, particularly the princesses who achieved great marriages even though exiled.

Exile is always a tough time to face, however, doing so with a brood of children who suddenly have little or no future, is even more difficult a task. At least, the Sicilians owned the vast Palazzo Farnese in Rome, where they soon settled under the protection of Pope Pius IX. And yet, finding the many children of the late King Ferdinando II a station in life became a matter of considerable importance.

Queen Maria Sophia of the Two Sicilies.

The first to seek some sort of settlement was the Count of Trani, Prince Luigi, eldest child of Ferdinando II and Maria Theresa. Luigi, who had valiantly supported his half-brother during the last dark days of the Sicilian monarchy, headed to Munich. There, he married in June 1861 Duchess Mathilde in Bavaria, a sister of Queen Maria Sophia. The bride, much like all her sisters, cherished the outdoors and always looked for stimulation, whether in the arts or in her interactions with people. Trani, as much as he tried, simply failed to meet her expectations. Although they did manage to produce one child, Maria Theresa (1867-1909), the marriage collapsed and the couple led respectfully separate lives. By then, Luigi was the heir to his half-brother Francesco II, and as such he expected to one day inherit, if not the throne, at the very least headship of house. That, however, never happened as the Count of Trani, afflicted by depression, committed suicide in 1886. During her long widowhood, the Countess of Trani spent long periods with her sisters, particularly Maria Sophia of the Two Sicilies and Empress Elisabeth of Austria. Three years after her husband's death, Mathilde safely settled her daughter by arranging for her marriage to Wilhelm, Fürst of Hohenzollern, and elder

Prince Gennaro of the Two Sicilies, Count of Caltagirone.

Prince Lodovico (Luigi), Count of Trani.

brother of King Ferdinand of Romania. The Countess of Trani survived her husband by early four decades. She died in Munich in June 1925.

Later that summer of 1861, Queen Maria Theresa settled her second daughter, Maria Immacolata, in the hands of Archduke Karl Salvator of Austria-Tuscany. The groom, born in Florence in 1839, was a first cousin of Maria Immacolata since his mother, Maria Antonietta, was a sister of King Ferdinando II. The Tuscan branch of the Habsburg dynasty had also lost its throne during the Risorgimento. However, given their connections with the Imperial Court in Vienna, Emperor Franz Joseph aided his relations and welcomed them to settle within the borders of his vast realm. Maria Immacolata and Karl Salvator had ten children, four died young, one at the age of twenty-five (Albrecht Salvator), while the remaining five reached adulthood. These included: Maria Theresa (1862-1933), who married her cousin Archduke Karl Stefan of Austria (1860-1933); Leopold Salvator (1863-1931), who married Infanta Blanca of Spain (1868-1949), one of the daughters of the Duke of Madrid, the leader of the last

Princess Mathilde, Countess of Trani.

Maria Theresa with daughter Auguste Viktoria (Queen of Portugal).

Carlist War; Franz Salvator (1866-1939), whose first wife was Archduchess Marie Valerie of Austria (1868-1924), youngest child of Emperor Franz Joseph; Carolina (1869-1945), who married Prince August Leopold of Saxe-Coburg & Gotha (1867-1922), a grandson of Emperor Pedro II and Empress Teresa Cristina of Brazil; and Maria Immakulata (1878-1968), who married Duke Robert of Württemberg (1873-1947).

Archduke Karl Salvator began serving in the Tuscan military during the Risorgimento. Later, once settled in Austria with his parents, he entered the Imperial Army. Besides serving with distinction, he was an inventor of considerable note, one of his creations improving the rifles used by the Austro-Hungarian army. Another of his patented inventions was a machine gun that was produced by the Skoda factories. Archduke Karl Salvator, who maintained homes in Vienna (the Palais Toskana), Bohemia and Gmunden, near Lake Traun, passed away in Vienna in January 1892. Archduchess Maria Immacolata, nicknamed "Petite," was quite popular at court in Vienna. It is said that Empress Elisabeth, envious of Maria Immacolata's acceptance in society, *"disdainfully referred to the family as the "pearl fishers," due to Emperor Franz Joseph's habit of presenting Maria Immacolata with a pearl necklace on the birth of each child."* Maria Immacolata died in Vienna in February 1899.

Princess Maria Immacolata, Archduchess Karl Salvator of Austria-Tuscany.

The next of the Sicilian siblings to settle down was Princess Maria Annunziata, who in 1863 landed a spectacularly advantageous groom, Archduke Karl Ludwig of Austria, brother of Emperor Franz Joseph, who had always remained deeply loyal to his Sicilian cousins and allies. Unlike their two other brothers, Karl Ludwig never gave the Emperor much worry. Not interested in politics, Archduke Karl Ludwig fulfilled his military duty, did what was expected, never questioned his brother's authority and whenever possible went on long journeys abroad, the source of much enjoyment to him. He was deeply interested in antiquities and became a patron of the arts. The third son of Archduke Franz Karl and his Bavarian wife Sophie, Karl Ludwig never expected he would one day become his older brother's immediate heir. This was so after the suicide of Crown Prince Rudolf in 1889. Archduke Karl Ludwig was not destined to inherit the throne after all. In 1896 he traveled on pilgrimage to the Holy Land and while there contracted an illness after drinking water from the River Jordan. He died in Vienna later that year, thus clearing the way for his eldest son, Archduke Franz Ferdinand to become the Empire's immediate heir, a position he held until his assassination June 1914.

Maria Annunziata, however, did not live long enough to see her son advance up the line of succession. The year

Archduke Karl Salvator and Archduchess Maria Immacolata of Austria-Tuscany.

following her wedding, Maria Annunziata gave birth to the couple's first child, Franz Ferdinand. Otto followed in 1865 and three years later she gave birth to a third son, Ferdinand Karl. By then her health was compromised by tuberculosis and by the time she gave birth to her fourth child, Margarete Sophie, Maria Annunziata was spent. She never truly recovered from her last pregnancy and the much-beloved "Ciolla," as she was called by the family, passed away in May 1871.

Six years after Maria Annunziatta's wedding, it was the turn of her brother Gaetano, Count of Girgenti. He also made a spectacular dynastic alliance to Infanta Isabel of Spain, eldest daughter of Queen Isabel II. Interestingly, although an act of renunciation of his Sicilian rights was drafted, Girgenti was not asked to sign it since at the time of his marriage the Prince of Asturias stood between Infanta Isabel and the throne. Had she succeeded to the throne, Girgenti would have had to renounce his Sicilian rights. This situation would happen again, but in that case when Prince Carlo married the Princess of Asturias, he was asked to sign a renunciation known as the Act of Cannes, a document that later would bring untold argument between various branches of the Sicilian Royal family and their supporters. Anyhow, couple married in Madrid in May 1868 and left immediately on their honeymoon. They were still traveling around when news of the revolution that toppled the Spanish queen reached the couple. Gaetano immediately traveled to Spain to join the forces attempting to save his mother-in-law's shaky throne. Once there, he participated in several skirmishes always leading his troops while yelling, *"Hurrah my Mother-in-law!"* The supporters of the Queen were defeated and Girgenti was captured and expelled from Spain.

He had already served in the Austrian Imperial army, and later wore Papal uniform. However, as the final confrontation between the Vatican and the Piedmontese approached, all Sicilian princes were forced to lay down their arms as fighting against the Savoys, per prior agreement, would put at risk any property still owned by the Sicilian Royal Family in the Papal States. Given

Archduke Karl Salvator of Austria-Tuscany.

Princess Maria Annunziata.

Archduke Karl Ludwig of Austria and his wife, Maria Annunziata.

that these properties included both the Palazzo Farnese and the Villa Caprarola, as well as the artwork decorating both buildings, Francesco II and his family could ill afford to lose these last remaining possessions.

The Count of Girgenti was an honorable man who lacked interest in politics. When he received his wife's immense dowry, Girgenti asked Isabel to reduce their expenditures so they could live on his much smaller budget. He did not want anyone to think that he had married for money. Theirs was not a love match either and one is left to wonder how they would have fared had he lived longer.

Sadly, there was little that Girgenti could do and not surprisingly idleness

Maria Annunziata and sons Archdukes Franz Ferdinand and Otto of Austria.

only contributed to his overall sense of despondency. Gaetano Girgenti suffered from various illnesses, epilepsy among them. He never recovered from the Spanish experience. Despondent and exhausted, in November 1871 the Count of Girgenti finally brought his suffering to an end. Infanta Isabel never remarried. She eventually returned to Spain after the restoration of her brother King Alfonso XII and served as the first lady of the Spanish court for several years. She was, in due time, the most loyal supporter of the Spanish monarchy. When the Caserta sons sought careers in Spain's military, their Aunt Infanta Isabel granted them her undivided support. She died in April 1931, soon after reaching Paris, having left Spain when her nephew King Alfonso XIII was ousted from the throne.

The second wedding the Sicilians celebrated in 1868 was that of Prince Alfonso, Count of Caserta, and his first cousin Princess Maria Antonietta of Bourbon-Two Sicilies. Since this couple forms the epicenter of this book, their life is discussed in Chapter V.

Princess Maria della Grazie Pia of Bourbon-Two Sicilies, the eighth child of King Ferdinando II and Queen Maria Theresa, married in 1869. Her groom, although not seated on a throne, was the exiled Duke of Parma, Roberto I. While he may have lost his throne, Roberto was one of the richest princes of his time, his properties spanning several countries and including several large estates in Italy, Austria-Hungary, Switzerland and France. He was the eldest son of Duke Carlo III, who was assassinated in 1854, and of his long-suffering wife, the former Princess Louise Marie of France, who once was mentioned as a bride for the Count of Lecce, King Ferdinando II's sickly brother. Roberto I and Maria Pia became parents in 1870, when she gave birth to a daughter, Princess Maria Luisa, who later would go on to marry future King Ferdinand of Bulgaria. The Dukes of Parma had eleven further children, but tragedy affected several of them as they were born mentally handicapped. In fact, of the couple's five sons only the fourth, Elias, left

Prince Gaetano, Count of Girgenti.

descendants from his marriage to Archduchess Maria Anna of Austria. One of them is the Infanta Alicia, the mother of Infante Carlos, Duke of Calabria. Two of the remaining four sons: Ferdinando died before his first birthday; Enrico and Giuseppe were mentally handicapped; and Augusto was born and died on the same day in 1882, his difficult birth being responsible for Maria Pia's death a week later. Besides Maria Luisa, the Dukes of Parma had six other daughters: four were affected in several degrees by the malady that kept two of their brothers in childlike existence; one only live a few weeks; one, Beatrice, married Count Pietro Luchesi Palli, a grandson by her second husband of Maria Carolina Ferdinanda, former Duchess de Berry.

Princess Maria Luisa was the last of the sisters to marry. Her choice fell on Prince Enrico of Bourbon-Parma, Count of Bardi, and their wedding was celebrated in Cannes in November 1873. Enrico, also a fairly wealthy young man, was the younger brother of the Duke of Parma. The couple went to Egypt on their honeymoon and while there she contracted fever. Five months after their wedding, the newlyweds landed in France where doctors who examined Maria Luisa realized her condition was alarming. The couple traveled to Cauterets, whether the sulphur waters were expected to aid the invalid princess.

Infanta Isabel of Spain, wife of the Count of Girgenti.

Even though they stopped at the Sanctuary of our Lady of Lourdes on their way, very little could be done to save Maria Luisa. She died in Pau, on the northern edge of the Pyrenees, on August 24, 1874. She was laid to rest in the chapel of the Villa Borbone, near Viareggio, Italy.

The only one of the Sicilian siblings to enter a non-royal marriage was Prince Pasquale, Count of Bari. He married a lady of French extraction by the name of Blanche Marconnay. She was four years her husband's senior and the family did not welcome the alliance. Their union proved childless and Pasquale nearly disappeared from the family's history after his wedding. He died in 1904. Mademoiselle Marconnay survived her princely husband until 1926. Both are buried in Montmartre Cemetery in Paris.

From left: Princesses Maria Pia, Maria Immacolata, Maria Luisa and Maria Annunziata of the Two Sicilies.

The Duke and Duchess of Parma, Roberto I and Maria Pia.

The Count of Bardi and
his second wife, Princess
Adelgunde of Bragança.

Prince Pasquale, Count of Bari.

Prince Pasquale, Count of Bari, earlier in his youth.

*Archduke Otto of Austria with his wife Maria Josepha and their two
sons, the future Emperor Karl I and Archduke Maximilian. Archduke
Otto was a grandson of King Ferdinando II of the Two Sicilies.*

SECTION *II*

The Children of King Ferdinando II

By his first wife Princess Maria Cristina of Savoy (1812-1836):

1.   H.M. King Francesco II of the Two Sicilies.
Born at Naples, January 16th 1836.
Married 1859 Duchess Maria Sophia in Bavaria.
Died at Arco, December 27th 1894.
Issue : 1 daughter.

By his second wife Archduchess Maria Theresa of Austria (1816-1867):

2.   Prince Ludovico (Luigi) Maria, Count of Trani.
Born at Naples, August 1st 1838.
Married 1861 Duchess Mathilde in Bavaria.
Died at Paris, June 8th 1886.
Issue : 1 daughter.

3.   Prince Alberto Maria Francesco, Count of Castrogiovanni.
Born at Capodimonte, September 17th 1839.
Died at Naples, July 12th 1844.

4.   PRINCE ALFONSO MARIA GIUSEPPE ALBERT, COUNT OF CASERTA.
Born at Caserta, March 28th 1841.
Died at Cannes, May 26th 1934.

5.   Princess Maria Annunziata Isabella Filomena Sabasia.
Born at Caserta, March 24th 1843.
Married 1862 Archduke Karl Ludwig of Austria.
Died at Vienna, May 4th 1871.
Issue : 4 children.

6.   Princess Maria Immacolata Clementina.
Born at Naples, April 14th 1844.
Married 1861 Archduke Karl Salvator of Austria-Tuscany.
Died at Vienna, February 18th 1899.
Issue : 10 children.

7.   Prince Gaetano Maria Federico, Count of Girgenti.
Born at Naples, January 12th 1846.

Married 1868 Infanta Isabel of Spain.
Died at Lucerne, November 26th 1871.

8.   Prince Giuseppe Maria, Count of Lucera.
Born at Naples, March 4th 1848.
Died at Portici, September 28th 1851.

9.   Princess Maria delle Grazie Pia.
Born at Gaeta, August 2nd 1849.
Married 1869 Duke Roberto I of Parma
Died at Biarritz, September 29th 1882.
Issue : 12 children.

10.   Prince Vincenzo Maria, Count of Melazzo.
Born at Naples, April 27th 1851.
Died at Caserta, October 14th 1854.

11.   Prince Pasquale, Count of Bari.
Born at Caserta, September 15th 1852.
Married 1878 Blanche de Marconnay.
Died at La Malmaison, Deceember 21st 1904.
No issue.

12.   Princess Maria Immaculata Luisa.
Born at Naples, January 21st 1855.
Married 1873 Prince Enrico of Bourbon-Parma, Count of Bardi.
Died at Pau, August 23rd 1874.
No issue.

13.   Prince Gennaro Maria Immaculata Luigi, Count of Caltagirone.
Born at Caserta, February 28th 1857.
Died at Albano, August 14th 1867.

CHAPTER *IV*

Francesco II
"A Last Stand at Gaeta"

*I*f history has been harsh in dealing with King Ferdinando II, it has been compassionate with King Francesco II, an unlucky and unfortunate monarch, whose undoubted qualities and good intentions were casualties of events beyond his control.

The only son by Ferdinando's first marriage, Francesco, born in 1836, grew up with a swarm of half-siblings under the gaze of his stepmother Maria Theresa, who although fond of her stepson, wished to further the fortunes of her own children. Hence, the Queen had no time for him and woefully neglected his education and development. Some argue that she lost no opportunity to denigrate him and was ambitious for her own sons, notably the eldest Luigi, Count of Trani, who, if anything had happened to Francesco, was next in line for the throne. As a result of his abject childhood Francesco grew up to be stammeringly shy and with no self-confidence whatsoever, and was intellectually not up to the tasks that awaited him as sovereign. While his accession in 1859 went smoothly, but there were already storm clouds on the horizon, with the movement for Italian unification gathering momentum and the entire peninsula

King Francesco II.

seething with unrest. Francesco II was considerably influenced by his reactionary stepmother and by the camarilla of ultra conservatives who were in ascendancy at court.

Francesco had married a few months before his accession. The wife chosen for him was the pretty seventeen-year old Maria Sophia Duchess in Bavaria, daughter of Duke Max and Duchess Ludovika in Bavaria, and a younger sister of the Empress Elisabeth of Austria. Another sister, Mathilde, as mentioned in the previous chapter, married Francesco II's half-brother, the Count of Trani. Much more intelligent

A painting depicting King Francesco II and Queen Maria Sophis during the siege of Gaeta.

and spirited than her husband, Maria Sophia overshadowed him, but despite their youth and incompatibility, the first few years of their marriage were happy enough, although no children appeared.

Soon after succeeding his father, King Francesco II was confronted with the worrisome consequences brought about by the victories obtained from the Austrians by the Franco-Piedmontese alliance. Austria's defeat in Northern Italy not only lost her most of Lombardy and the city of Milan, but it also brought to an end her long and historical presence in Italy. With Vienna basically cut off from meddling in Italian affairs, her allies were now abandoned to their dire fate. The Dukes of Modena and Parma, as well as the Grand Duke of Tuscany were overthrown. In Naples, his prime minister advised joining the Savoys in an alliance against the papacy, but King Francesco II could not bring himself to do so because he considered this to be a heretical move. His Uncles Capua and Siracusa also recommended the same course of action, but their voices were drowned by the conservative camarilla that had the uppr hand at court.

The situation worsened when the Swiss Guard, the strongest bulwark of the dynasty, mutinied and demanded that the King address their many grievances. Instead

King Vittorio Emanuele II.

of pacifying this important branch of the Neapolitan army, one of Francesco II's generals surrounded the mutineers and shot them. As a result, the Swiss Guard was disbanded and the King of the Two Sicilies lost his most efficient regiment leaving the royal army considerably weakened. All around Francesco II conspiracies and rebellion presaged the fall of the kingdom and little could be done to prevent that outcome,

In May 1860, Garibaldi landed in the west of Sicily with an army of roughly 1000 Italian volunteers, the "Mille." They rapidly gained control of the island and the capital, Palermo, fell by the end of the month, Garibaldi claiming the island in the name of King Vittorio Emanuele of Sardinia. The rebel forces then turned their attention to the mainland and crossed the Straits of Messina into Naples' territory. Driving the King's forces back after several encounters, they made speedy progress and Garibaldi himself entered the city of Naples on September 7, 1860, declaring the Bourbons deposed.

Giuseppe Garibaldi.

Meanwhile, the Piedmontese, witnessing the quick disintegration of the Bourbon dynasty, lost no time in invading the Two Sicilies from the north and capturing the city of Capua.

King Francesco's troops fought on in rural areas, but were finally forced to retreat to the enormous coastal fortress of Gaeta. There, the victorious Piedmontese armies surrounded the last vestiges of the once mighty Kingdom of the Two Sicilies. Francesco II and his troops withstood a siege of over three months, during which time the spirited young Queen Maria Sophia earned a place in history for herself as "The Heroine of Gaeta." Showing remarkable sang-froid she appeared on the battlements to rally the troops under fire and tended to the sick and wounded. Her efforts were to no avail and after being starved into submission the garrison was forced to surrender. The King and Queen fled to the safety of Rome and placed themselves under the protection of Pope Pius IX.

King Francesco II of the Two Sicilies.

Among the possessions remaining to the King was the Palazzo Farnese in Rome, which had come to him by inheritance, and it was there the Royal Family took up residence. All their private possessions in their former Kingdom were confiscated without compensation. Francesco II and a group of loyalists set up a government-in-exile while in Rome and some of Europe's Catholic powers (including Spain, Austria and Bavaria) recognized it. However, after the Austro-Prussian War in 1866, facing further Piedmontese expansion in Italy, Francesco II finally gave up and departed Rome before it fell to the Savoys.

In the meantime, Maria Sophia became disillusioned with her life in Italy and it was during this period that she was rumored to have started an affair with a Belgian officer in the Papal Guard, resulting in the clandestine birth of a child in 1862, who was immediately adopted out.

After the death of Queen Maria Theresa in 1867, however, she and Francesco were reconciled. It seems that the King suffered from "phimosis," a medical condition that prevented him from successfully copulating. This problem was fixed after he underwent an operation to correct a malformation that prevented the King from consummating his

Opposite page: King Francesco II and Queen Maria Sophia of the Two Sicilies.

marriage. To their joy a child was born to them in Rome in 1870, a daughter called Maria Christina, in honor of her paternal grandmother, but the little girl lived only a few months.

Pope Pius IX.

After the fall of Rome the couple had to flee again and set up home in Paris. Their wandering existence also brought them to Bavaria and Austria, where Emperor Franz Joseph always treated his brother-in-law with full honors. Francesco II never renounced his rights to the Sicilian throne, nor did he accept any restitution from the Savoys. In exile, his main source of income was provided by the revenue coming from rents raised by the Palazzo Farnese, which he finally sold to the French government in 1874.

In exile, living a wandering and purposeless existence, Maria Sophia grew restless again and began to travel extensively – the couple was separated in all but name, but a strong bond always existed between them. King Francesco never gave up hope of regaining his throne and blamed his misfortunes on his youth and inexperience. He died at Arco, in the South Tyrol, then part of the Austro-Hungarian Empire in 1894 as a result of complications from diabetes. A contemporary remembered the exiled King as, *"admirable in his conduct, both as a man and as a husband."* Francesco II possessed a *"gentle dignity"* responsible for winning him *"universal respect."* Furthermore, *"Until his death he continued to protest that he was Neapolitan in heart and soul, and to express a hungry interest in all the news that reached him from his former kingdom."*

The last King of the Two Sicilies died convinced that his subjects, in spite

Queen Maria Sophia, the "heroine of Gaeta."

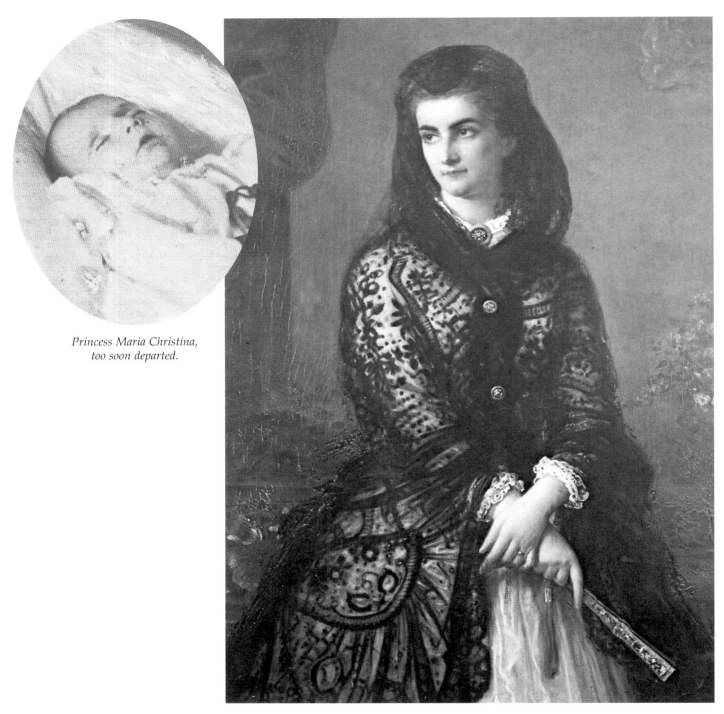

*Princess Maria Christina,
too soon departed.*

Queen Maria Sophia of the Two Sicilies.

of events, had remained loyal to him. He lived in exile for thirty-four years in am ambiance of *"melancholy and resignation,"* forgiving those who betrayed him, but protesting against the *"sorrow and falsehood"* that had become part of the *"contemporary scene."* The year before his death, Francesco II best expressed his despondency with current affairs by writing, *"May God will that from this period of dark confusion, toward which we are approaching, another very different period will emerge, of reparation and rectification of wrongs suffered, granting all of us strength to bear the former and make the best use of the latter."* "You tell me that patience makes a martyr of man," he wrote to an old friend just before his death, *"I sincerely hope so for the sake of my soul, but I do not count much on it, considering our fragility and that of the human factors on which we depend."*

King Francesco II and Queen Maria Sophia of the Two Sicilies.

When news of her husband's untimely death reached her in Paris, where they had resided for quite some time, Maria Sophia rushed to Arco to be present at the funeral ceremony. A bevy of Sicilian royalty, supported by many Habsburgs and Bavarian relations, as well as the Duke of Parma and the Hereditary Prince of Hohenzollern, attended the five hour-long funeral. Several Neapolitan and Sicilian nobles were in attendance, while *"two battalions of Tyrolese cuirassiers"* escorted the King's body. *"The Archbishop of Trento officiated, and the drums of an Austrian regiment rolled in honor of the departed monarch while guns boomed in the distance, like to echoes of those at Gaeta,"* wrote a noted historian.

After laying her husband to rest, Maria

Queen Maria Sophia in later years.

Sophia returned to their home in Neuilly-sur-Seine, an elegant suburb of Paris. Unlike many a widow, she continued traveling and indulging in the physical exercise that had made women of her family famous. She frequently joined her sisters Mathilde Trani and Elisabeth as they traveled tirelessly from one corner of the continent to the other. She was an avid equestrian and rode her beautiful horses nearly every day. Tragedy, never far away from the Wittelbachs and Sicilians, made its unforgiving presence soon after Francesco II's death. In 1897, Maria Sophia's sister, Sophie, Duchess d'Alençon, met a horrific death after being burnt alive in a fire at the Charity Bazaar in Paris. The following year, their elder sister, Elisabeth of Austria met an untimely end by falling victim to

In Arco, South Tyrol, a royal group gathers, From left: King Francesco II of the Two Sicilies; Archduke Albrecht of Austria, Duke of Teschen; Prince Alfonso, Count of Caserta (King Francesco II's half-brother and heir); and Princess Maria Immacolata, the Count of Caserta's daughter.

Empress Elisabeth of Austria.

an assassin's blade as she boarded a ferry in Geneva. It seemed as if destiny would not spare the ageing Neapolitan queen anything, yet she *"never pitied herself – She desired nothing from the past and had long ceased to count on the future."* The comfort she failed to find in the company of humans, she more than discovered surrounded by her beloved horses.

Maria Sophia survived King Francesco II for over thirty years, a legendary figure from a bygone era, moving at the outset of World War I from Paris to her homeland of Bavaria. She remained, throughout her long life, a convinced enemy of the Savoy Kingdom of Italy. Some of her critics even went as far as accusing her of playing a part in the conspiracy that led to the assassination of King Umberto I in 1900. Later, during the Great War, she was accused of sabotage and espionage against Italy. All of these were rumors, as no evidence exists of her involvement in any plot. Such

however, such was her fame, that she developed a cult-like group of followers who believed she was capable of anything Maria Sophia set her mind to. Even noted Italian poet Gabriele D'Annunzio called her the *"stern little Bavarian eagle."*

One of the last vestiges of a bygone era, Queen Maria Sophia died in Munich in 1925. Her remains laid there for nearly six decades until in 1984 the King and Queen and their infant daughter were reinterred in the Basilica of Santa Chiara in Naples.

King Francesco II in old age.

Princess Sophie d'Orléans, Duchess d'Alençon.

Princess Mathilde, Countess of Trani.

47

CHAPTER V

The Count and Countess of Caserta: Alfonso & Antonietta

Born at the imposing Palace of Caserta on March 28, 1841, Prince Alfonso Maria Giuseppe Alberto of the Two Sicilies, titled Count of Caserta by his father, inherited no elevated position at his birth, being merely the third son of King Ferdinando II of the Two Sicilies by his second wife Archduchess Maria Theresa of Austria, and the fourth son altogether, as Ferdinando had another older son, Crown Prince Francesco, by his first wife Princess Christina of Savoy. After him came another nine siblings, four daughters and five sons. All the children grew up in an atmosphere commensurate to their position as nineteenth century royalty — surrounded by courtiers, privately educated, moving between various of the family's residences and early military training for the boys, art, painting and languages for the girls. Their private family life was exemplary. Whatever other charges can be leveled against King Ferdinando II he was a devoted husband and father and spent a great amount of time in the company of his children. His wife Queen Maria Theresa was a full-time mother with little time for social obligations and of an extremely pious nature. In 1844 Alfonso's elder brother Prince Alberto, Count of Castrogiovanni, died at the age of 4, moving him one place up the line of succession.

As a teenager Alfonso could only watch as political events unfolded in his homeland following his father's death and the accession of his half-brother as King Francesco II. At the age of ten, Caserta began his military career when

The Countess of Trapani and her daughter, Princess Maria Antonietta, who in 1868 married her first cousin the Count of Caserta.

Opposite page: The Count of Caserta during the last days of the Sicilian monarchy.

he was, *"enrolled as a banner bearer of the III Regiment of the Line of the Two Sicilies."* Two years later he was promoted to "alfieri," and by 1857 he had become 1st lieutenant. The following year he became captain and when his brother succeeded to the throne in 1859, Caserta became his aide-de-camp. That same year, since he had studied the subject at military college, Alfonso was transferred to the artillery. All the while, the kingdom prepared for the imminent invasion that Garibaldi and his Savoy allies were

The Count and Countess of Caserta.

planning. The kingdom, its institutions and the military, as well as the common folk still loyal to the dynasty knew what incorporation into Italy would mean the disappearance of independence and subjugation to a Northern Italian kingdom under the rule of the Savoy. Everyone knew what was at stake.

The Count of Caserta and his brother the Count of Trapani in military uniform.

When Garibaldi invaded, the Count of Caserta was in command of two batteries firing the Savoy armies near Capua. By October 1860, when with his brother Trani he fought in the battle to recapture Caiazzo Caserta had already been promoted to lieutenant colonel. Witnesses later recalled that both royal brothers fought with great distinction. Later that month he was promoted to colonel and Caserta fought at Garigliano, where in recognition of his bravery he was awarded the cross of officer of the Order of St George of the Reunion. Caserta participated in the Siege of Gaeta, mentioned before, and shared the fate of the rest of his family when the Kingdom of the Two Sicilies ceased to exist. The Count of Caserta's bravery at Gaeta was not only recognized by those who served with him, but also by other European sovereigns, like Queen Isabel II of Spain, Emperor Franz Joseph of Austria and tTsar Alexander II of Russia, who conferred various orders on him.

Other members of the Royal Family followed the King and Queen into exile and took up residence in Rome, at the Palazzo Farnese. It was at the Vatican, in 1868, that Alfonso married his 17 year-old first cousin Maria Antonietta, daughter of his uncle the Count of Trapani by his Habsburg wife Archduchess Maria Isabella. The Pope himself conducted the wedding with great pomp and ceremony, and Maria Antonietta brought a considerable dowry with her to the marriage, most useful to the family, as Alfonso, being a younger son, was not heir to any large fortune. All the family's Sicilian possessions had been confiscated, and apart from the Palazzo Farnese, there were only a few remaining properties remaining to them from the Farnese inheritance.

In 1870 the Franco-Prussian War broke out, and Emperor Napoleon III removed all his troops from Rome, no longer providing protection to the Papal States. Diplomatic attempts were made to persuade Pope Pius IX to come to a settlement but he would have none of it. The Italian Army laid siege to the city and on September 20, 1870, they finally breached the walls and entered the city. After a quickly arranged plebiscite Rome was annexed to the Kingdom of Italy at the beginning of October. The Pope declared himself a prisoner in the Vatican, his temporal power removed and his territories lost, and it was not until 1929 that the Papacy concluded a Concordat with the Italian Government and the House of Savoy.

With the fall of Rome, the Two Sicilies Royal Family was homeless again. The King and Queen went to Austria, whilst the Casertas spent a short period of time in Switzerland, going on from there to the South Tyrol region of Austria, where their second son Carlo(s) was born at Gries near Bolzano in 1870, then to Schloß Frohsdorf, Austrian residence of the Count of Chambord and from there to Vienna, where they were well received by the Emperor Franz Joseph and their numerous Austrian relatives. The Count of Caserta, whose education was compromised by the military requirements he faced from a young age, now found that life, once again, lacked purpose. He pained for something to do and the worsening political situation in the Iberian Peninsula soon enough gave him a cause to defend.

The Countess of Caserta.

Meanwhile, in Spain turmoil ruled unquestioned. Queen Isabella II had been dethroned in a coup d'état and replaced as Spain's monarch by the Savoyard Duke of Aosta, who reigned briefly as Amedeo I until abdicating in February 1873, after which Spain was declared a Republic. Young, and exiled, Infante Carlos of Spain, Duke of Madrid, and husband of Princess Margherita of Bourbon-Parma, a niece of the Count de Chambord, convinced of his inalienable rights to the throne, arrived in Spain in 1872 to lead his troops in the Third Carlist War. The Count of Caserta, chafing with the inactivity of exile decided to join the campaign and was joined in this mission by his brothers-in-law the Duke of Parma and the Count of Bardi, and the three Princes were appointed generals. The war continued with considerable ferocity across Northern Spain throughout 1873 and 1874. In December of the latter year however leading Spanish army officers proclaimed Alfonso, the Prince of Asturias, son of the deposed Queen Isabel II as King of Spain and he arrived back in January 1875. The restoration provoked a marked change of heart by the Count of Caserta, who reconciled with the family of the new King and returned to France. The Third Carlist War in Spain continued until late 1876 ending in defeat for the Duke of Madrid. It was the last of the Carlist uprisings.

The Count of Caserta urgently needed a permanent home and wanted to be near the Mediterranean and after a further period of searching, eventually chose Cannes on the French Riviera to be the family's future place of residence. To raise some necessary funds the Palazzo Farnese in Rome was leased out to the French Government and eventually became the French Embassy in Italy. As luck would have it, a lottery ticket in his possession brought the Count of Caserta an unexpected windfall. With

In back, from left: Maria Christina, Gennaro, Ferdinando-Pio holding Filippo, Maria Pia, Carlo, Maria Immacolata. Seated, at front in the same order: Prince Ranieri and Princess Maria Giuseppina, c. 1886.

his share of the revenue from the rent of the Palazzo Farnese, he acquired a large residence on the seafront, which was baptized Villa Marie-Thérèse in honor of his late mother. The house was of imposing proportions and surrounded by extensive gardens and was large enough to accommodate the ever-increasing family (a third son Francesco had been born in 1873) plus a large domestic staff, including some loyal retainers who had followed the family into exile. It also contained a private chapel, as the family were devoutly Catholic, where Mass was said every morning.

At this period in time Cannes was an up-and-coming holiday resort and many noble and wealthy families had luxurious property there. Russian Grand Dukes were frequent visitors and the Grand Duchess of Mecklenburg-Schwerin, born Grand Duchess Anastasia Mikhailovna of Russia, lived there semi-permanently with her children. For the next fifty years the Villa Marie-Thérèse was the focal point of family life for the Casertas, who rapidly filled it with a further succession of children – Maria Immacolata was born in 1874, Maria Christina in 1877, Maria Pia in 1878, Maria Giuseppina in 1880, Gennaro in 1882, Ranieri in 1883, Filippo in 1885, Francesco d'Assissi in 1888 and finally Gabriele in 1897, when his mother was almost 46 years of age. The children led a fairly carefree existence at the villa – the beach was just across the road and there was a tennis court in the

grounds, but considerable time and effort was put into their education as well. Their personal lifestyle was largely frugal, as lack of funds remained, always, a constant problem.

The Count of Caserta.

In 1886 the Count of Caserta's eldest brother Luigi, Count of Trani, committed suicide in Paris at the age of 47, leaving only a daughter, Princess Maria Teresa, later Princess of Hohenzollern, by his marriage to Duchess Mathilde in Bavaria, a younger sister of Queen Maria Sophia. This was the second brother Caserta lost to suicide since Prince Gaetano, Count of Girgenti, took his own life in 1871. Gaetano had made a dynastic marriage with his cousin Infanta Isabel of Spain, eldest daughter of Queen Isabel II. The widowed Countess Girgenti cherished her husband's memory so very much that she was never interested in marrying again. Instead, she became one of the pillars of the Alphonsine monarchy reestablished with the ascension to the throne of her brother King Alfonso XII whose daughter, María de las Mercedes, Girgenti's nephew, Prince Carlo, would wed in 1901 – the never-ending wheels of the old royal marriage system never stopped turning and eventually coming full circle. Infanta Isabel, as it also turned out, was very supportive of her Sicilian in-laws when the Casertas sent their sons to serve in the Spanish army.

Princesses Maria Pia, Maria Christina and Maria Giuseppina.

Anyhow, the Count of Trani's death advanced the Count of Caserta's position to that of immediate heir and successor to his childless half-brother King Francesco II. By then, it became imperative to find the Caserta sons an acceptable station in life. Foremost, the brothers had to undergo military careers. Spain, where Caserta's first cousin Maria Cristina of Austria served as regent for her infant son Alfonso XIII, seemed an appropriate destination for his sons. Furthermore, as descendants of the former Infanta Maria Isabel, Caserta's Spanish grandmother, all his sons held dynastic rights in Spain, even though these were quite remote. In order to begin a dialogue, King Francesco II sent a formal letter to Maria Cristina requesting the admission of his nephews Ferdinand-Pius and Carlo to Spanish military schools. As she always wanted to assist relations fallen on hard times, the Queen Regent consented to the request. In 1891, when the princes graduated from military school, the Count of Caserta asked his cousin the Queen Regent to permit his sons to make their career in the Spanish military and be accorded Spanish nationality. King Francesco II, who added a letter expressing his support for his brother's letter,

Standing in back, from left: the Count of Caserta, Prince Filippo, Prince Friedrich Christian of Saxony, Prince Rainier and Prince Gennaro. At front, same order: Princess Johann Georg of Saxony, the Countess of Caserta, King Friedrich August III of Saxony and Princess Maria Giuseppina.

The Count and Countess of Caserta in old age.

The Caserta children posing outside the Villa Marie Thérèse, from left: Ferdinando-Pio, Francesco di Pola, Maria Christina, Carlo(s), Ranieri, Maria Immacolata, Gennaro, Maria Pia, Maria Giuseppina and Filippo. Seated at front: Gabriele.

sent Caserta's petition to Maria Cristina. The King, however, also negotiated with the Spanish government an agreement that allowed his nephews to retain both their titles and rank while serving in the Spanish military.

King Francesco himself died in Austria in 1894, and Alfonso succeeded him as Head of the Royal House of the Two Sicilies, immediately issuing a proclamation maintaining his right to the throne. His succession brought him very little in the way of material possessions – the widowed Queen Maria Sophia had to be taken care of, and of the Italian properties from the Farnese inheritance little remained. Another pressing problem for the Count was the future of his children remaining. It was to be hoped that the girls would find good husbands amongst other Royal Catholic families in Europe, but the boys were more of a problem. In exile, with limited resources and no estates to administer, the military seemed the best option. Alfonso turned again to his

The Countess of Caserta surrounded by her daughters: Maria Immacolata, Maria Giuseppina, Maria Christina and Maria Pia.

The Villa Marie-Thérèse, Cannes.

cousin in Spain, the Queen Regent Maria Cristina, for assistance. This connection to the Queen Regent of Spain is best understood when looking at their shared genealogy: the Count of Caserta and the Queen Regent of Spain were first cousins. The Count's mother, Maria Theresa, was the eldest sister of Archduke Karl Ferdinand of Austria, Queen Regent Maria Cristina's father. Maria Theresa and Karl Ferdinand were the siblings of the very prominent, and extremely wealthy Archduke Albrecht, Duke of Teschen, the right-hand military advisor of Emperor Franz Joseph. Hence, Queen Regent Maria Cristina was well disposed toward the family and was prepared to offer positions in the Spanish armed forces to the younger Sicilian Princes as well. Hence, with the exception of young Prince Francesco di Paolo, who did not enjoy good health, all the Caserta sons eventually made their way to Madrid to serve under the Spanish crown. This gave them not only an occupation and an income, but also a purpose in life.

Meanwhile, at the Villa Marie-Thérèse life continued in a timeless fashion. A constant stream of children and relations came and went, and loyal supporters from the former Kingdom would make the journey from the south of Italy to pay their respects to the Count of Caserta. The house was the focal point for the whole family, and the constantly increasing number of grandchildren arrived regularly to spend a holiday at the seaside with "Nonno" and "Nonna." Births and marriages came one after the other and even death visited the family in 1914 when the young Prince Francesco di Paolo, who had developed tuberculosis, died in a sanatorium at Montreux in Switzerland. The villa came through the First World War relatively unscathed, but the aftermath brought many vicissitudes to the younger members of the family – the loss of thrones in Germany and Austria led to loss of status, income and in some cases to exile, and also to the untimely death of the Caserta's son-in-law Prince Luiz of Orléans-Bragança. The Count had also been forced for economic reasons to dispose of another of the last few Farnese properties belonging to the family, the Villa Madama on the outskirts of Rome, which now provides accommodation for official visitors to the Italian state.

The Royal Family's finances were a constant source of worry and complication. The Savoy Kingdom of Italy never compensated the Bourbons of the Two Sicilies

The Countess of Caserta in old age.

The 90th birthday of the Count of Caserta, 1931. Back row: Prince Gabriele, Infante Alfonso of Spain, Prince Gennaro, Infante Carlos of Spain, Princesses María and Dolores of Bourbon-Two Sicilies, Prince Johann Georg of Saxony, Duke Philipp-Albrecht of Württemberg, Count Jan Zamoyski, Duchess Rosa of Württemberg, Archduke Gottfried of Austria-Tuscany, Prince Ranieri, unidentified, Princess Antonietta, Prince Filippo, Odette Labori, Archduke Peter Ferdinand of Tuscany, Princess Lucia, Countess Teresa Zamoyska and Princess Maria Christina. Seated, same order: Infanta Isabel Alfonsa of Spain, Princess Carolina, Infanta Luisa of Spain, Countess Carolina Zamoyska, the Duchess of Calabria, the Countess of Caserta with Count Carlos Zamoyski, the Count of Caserta with Prince Antonio, Princess Johann Georg of Saxony, Archduchess Maria Christina of Austria-Tuscany, Princess Maria Pia d'Orléans-Bragança, Princess Maria Giuseppina and Beatrice Bordessa. On the floor, same order: Princesses Carmen, Urraca, Esperanza, Princess Pia and Prince Pedro Henrique d'Orléans-Bragança, Prince Carlos and Prince Ferdinando, Prince Luis–Gastão d'Orléans-Bragança, and Archduke Georg of Austria-Tuscany.

for the property they had lost in 1860. The properties the family still owed in the former Papal States and in Rome was eventually sold. Artwork was sold as finances required. In 1911 the Palazzo Farnese was sold to France for 3,400,000 francs, a considerable sum at the time, but this had to be shared by several stakeholders, among them Caserta, Queen Maria Sophia, the children of Fürstin Maria Teresa of Hohenzollern and several other Sicilian princes and princesses. "The Count of Caserta, however, remained the owner of many of the works of art" that had decorated the Palazzo Farnese.

As the Casertas aged, the Villa Marie Thérèse itself was becoming a liability – too large for the family now, it was both increasingly expensive to maintain and beginning to fall into disrepair. After fifty years of occupancy the Count of Caserta sold it in 1926 to a development company that subsequently demolished it and constructed a luxury hotel in its place. The five-star Hotel Martinez now occupies the plot on the Croisette in Cannes. The Casertas moved to a smaller house, also in Cannes but further inland on the Route d'Antibes, which was promptly re-baptised – Villa Marie-Thérèse! This more manageable property was to remain the Caserta's home for the rest of their lives.

In 1918 they had celebrated their Golden Wedding, in 1928 their Diamond Wedding, and in 1933 their Iron Wedding – 65 years. Each of these occasions was marked by a huge family party attended by all the children and grandchildren, as was the 90th birthday of the Count in 1931. The aged Count was faced with further worry in 1931 when a Republic was declared in Spain and King Alfonso XIII went into exile, thus putting paid to the army and naval careers of various of his sons. At the age of 93 Alfonso died in May 1934, his wife following him four years later. The Countess of Caserta died at Freiburg in 1938 while visiting her daughter Immacolata. They are both buried in the family mausoleum in the cemetery of Grand Jas in Cannes.

THE CHILDREN OF THE COUNT & COUNTESS OF CASERTA

1.   H.R.H. Prince Ferdinando. Duke of Calabria.
Born at Rome, July 5th 1869.
Died at Lindau, January 7th 1960.
Married 1897 Princess Marie of Bavaria.
Born at Villa Amsee, July 6th 1872.
Died at Villa Amsee, June 10th, 1954.
Issue: 1 son & 5 daughters.

2.   H.R.H. Prince Carlo(s).
Born at Gries, November 20th 1870.
Died at Seville, November 11th 1949.
Married, 1st, 1901 Infanta María de las Mercedes of Spain, Princess of Asturias.
Born at Madrid, September 11th, 1880.
Died at Madrid, October, 17th 1904.
Issue: 2 sons & 1 daughter.
Married, 2nd, 1907 Princess Louise of Orléans.
Born at Cannes, February 24th, 1882.
Died: at Seville, April 18th, 1958.
Issue: 1 son & 3 daughters.

3.   H.R.H. Prince Francesco di Paolo.
Born at Cannes, July 14th 1873.
Died at Cannes, June 26th 1876.

4.   H.R.H. Princess Maria Immacolata.
Born at Cannes, October 30th 1874.
Died at Muri, November 28th 1947.
Married 1906 Prince Johann Georg of Saxony.
Born at Dresden, July 10th, 1869.
Died at Altshausen, November 24th, 1938.
No issue.

5.   H.R.H. Princess Maria Christina.
Born at Cannes, April 10th 1877.
Died at St. Gilgen, October 4th 1947.
Married 1900 Archduke Peter Ferdinand of Austria-Tuscany.
Born at Salzburg, May 12th, 1874.
Died at St. Gilgen, November 8, 1948.
Issue: 2 sons & 2 daughters.

6.   H.R.H. Princess Maria Pia.
Born at Cannes, August 12th 1878.
Died at Mandelieu, June 20th 1973.
Married 1908 Prince Luiz of Orléans-Bragança.
Born at Petropolis, January 26th 1878.
Died at Cannes, March 26th, 1920.
Issue: 2 sons & 1 daughter.

7.   H.R.H. Princess Maria Giuseppina.
Born at Cannes, March 25th 1880.
Died at Cannes, July 22nd 1971.

8.   H.R.H. Prince Gennaro.
Born at Cannes, January 24th 1882.
Died at Cannes, April 11th 1944.
Married 1922 Beatrice Dorothy Bordessa, "Countess of Villa Colli)
Born at Saltney, Cheshire, December 29th 1879.
Died at West Malling, August 20th, 1963.
No issue.

9.   H.R.H. Prince Ranieri. Duke of Castro.
Born at Cannes, December 3rd 1883.
Died at Roquebrune-sur-Argens, January 13th 1973.
Married 1923 Countess Karoline Zamoyska.
Born at Cracow, September 22nd 1896.
Died at Marseille, May 9th 1968.
Issue: 1 son & 1 daughter.

10.   H.R.H. Prince Filippo.
Born at Cannes, December 10th 1885.
Died at St. John, March 9th 1949.
Married, 1st, 1916 (annulled 1925) Princess Marie Louise of Orléans.
Born at Cannes, December 10th, 1885.
Died at New Brunswick, March 9th, 1949.
Issue: 1 son.
Married, 2nd, 1927 Odette Labori.
Born at Paris, November 22nd, 1902.
Died at Le Kremlin-Bicetre, June 19th 1968.
No Issue.

11.   H.R.H. Prince Francesco.
Born at Cannes, January 13th 1888.
Died at Montreux, March 26th 1914.

12.   H.R.H. Prince Gabriele.
Born at Cannes, January 11th 1897.
Died at Itu, October 22nd 1975.
Married, 1st, 1927 Princess Malgorzata Czartoriski
Born at Warsaw, August 17th, 1902.
Died at Cannes, March 8th 1929.
Issue: 1 son.
Married, 2nd, 1932 Princess Cecile Lubomirska.
Born at Poreba Wielka, June 28th 1907.
Died at São Paulo, September 20th, 2001.
Issue: 2 sons & 2 daughters.

CHAPTER VI

Ferdinando
Duke of Calabria

The first-born son, Ferdinando-Pio, known in the family circle as "Nando" was born at the Palazzo Farnese in 1869 and received the title traditionally borne by the heir to the throne of the Two Sicilies, Duke of Calabria.

After an early upbringing in Cannes, Ferdinando was sent to the Austrian Military Academy at Wiener Neustadt and received an officer's commission in the Austro-Hungarian Army. Later on, taking up the Queen Regent of Spain's offer he became an officer in the Spanish Army, where he served with distinction in the war between Spain and Cuba and also saw service in Spanish Morocco.

In 1897 Ferdinando married Princess Marie, second daughter of Prince Ludwig of Bavaria (future King Ludwig III) in Munich. For an exiled family with limited resources this was an ideal match, as Marie brought a dowry with her and also received an apanage as a Bavarian Princess. His bride was a niece of Queen Regent Maria Cristina of Spain, who had done so much for the Caserta siblings. Hence living in Spain under the watchful eye of the Regent, it is not surprising that both Calabria and his brother Carlos, who were held in the highest regard by all who knew them, would find suitable brides among Maria Cristina's closest relations.

The Duke of Calabria.

At the time of Ferdinando and Marie's wedding, her grandfather served as Prince Regent of Bavaria. In fact, the kingdom had been under a regency since 1886 when the madness of King Ludwig II led to his seclusion (he drowned in mysterious circumstances along with his doctor). Ludwig II's only brother, and the country's next monarch, King Otto, was mentally unstable as well and he was unable to rule. Consequently,

Opposite page: Prince Ferdinando-Pio, Duke of Calabria.

The Duke and Duchess of Calabria with their two eldest daughters: Maria Antonietta and Maria Cristina c. 1899.

their Uncle Luitpold, Princess Marie's grandfather, was placed in charge of the regency that last until his own death in 1912. At that time, his son Ludwig as Prince Regent succeeded Luitpold. By then, King Otto had been secluded for more than a quarter of a century and in 1913 the Prince Regent made the decision that it was time to accept fact and remove his mad cousin from the throne. Parliament sided with the new monarch, Ludwig III. By then, the Dukes of Calabria had settled in Munich, where now as the King's son-in-law Ferdinando-Pio enjoyed a prominent position in the Bavarian capital.

In spite of his prominent marriage in Bavaria, Calabria still served in the Spanish military. Hence, once the couple's honeymoon came to an end, they traveled to Spain, where the Queen Regent welcomed her niece with open arms. In 1898 Marie gave birth to the couple's first child, Maria Antonietta. The next child, Maria Cristina, named in honor of the Regent, was also born in Madrid. Then in 1901, Marie gave birth to the long-awaited heir, Prince Ruggiero. The next year, Marie gave birth to her fourth child in as many years. This time, however, the birthing took place in Munich. Barbara, as the princess was named, went on to be the first one in the family to marry. Two more daughters were to join the family in due course, Lucie (Lucia), born at Schloß Nymphenburg in 1908, and Urraca, born there as well in 1913.

The Dukes of Calabria and three of their daughters: Barbara, Maria Antonietta and Maria Cristina.

The Duke of Calabria became greatly attached to his German second home and was to spend the rest of his life there. He and his family were assigned an apartment at Schloß Nymphenburg, which they occupied until the fall of the Monarchy in 1918. They then purchased at townhouse in Munich that they lost to Allied bombs during the Second World War. Fortunately, they also had a summer residence, the Villa Amsee on the shores of Lake Constance near Lindau, and this became the permanent family home during the later years of their lives. The Villa, in fact, is still in the possession of members of the Bavarian Royal Family.

Ferdinando and Marie suffered a great personal tragedy when their only son and heir Prince

Opposite page:
The Duke
and Duchess
of Calabria.

Prnicess Maria Antonietta and Maria Cristina in 1915.

Ruggiero, handicapped from birth, died at the age of thirteen. They also showered their five daughters with love and attention, as this was a very happy family, in spite of the tragedies that life had in store for them – the eldest, Maria Antonietta, never married and was killed in a car crash in Switzerland in 1957. The second, Maria Christina, married late in life Dom Manuel Sotomayor y Luna, who had been a diplomat at the Holy See and subsequently elected Vice-President of the Republic of Ecuador. He died less than two years after the wedding and the widowed Princess thereafter split her life between Ecuador and Germany. Princess Maria Cristina died in Quito, the capital of Ecuador in 1985. The third daughter, Barbara, married Count Franz Xavier zu Stolberg-Wernigerode, member of a mediatized German Princely family and died giving birth to her fourth child in 1927. Their wedding was celebrated with considerable pomp at the Royal palace in Munich and provided the family with an opportunity to host many of their royal relations. Princess Lucia, the fourth daughter, married at Schloß Nymphenburg in 1938 Prince Eugenio of Savoy, Duke of Ancona – this wedding sealed a reconciliation between the Two Sicilies family and the Savoys and was

The Duke and Duchess of Calabria with four of their daughters: Maria Antonietta, Maria Cristina, Barbara and Lucia.

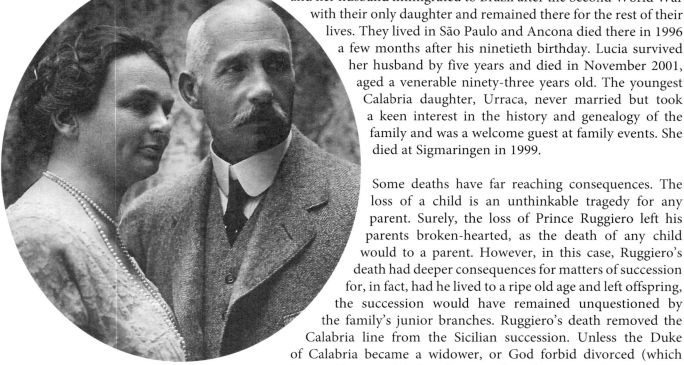

The Duke and Duchess of Calabria.

attended by Crown Prince Umberto of Italy, Prince of Piedmont. Lucia and her husband immigrated to Brazil after the Second World War with their only daughter and remained there for the rest of their lives. They lived in São Paulo and Ancona died there in 1996 a few months after his ninetieth birthday. Lucia survived her husband by five years and died in November 2001, aged a venerable ninety-three years old. The youngest Calabria daughter, Urraca, never married but took a keen interest in the history and genealogy of the family and was a welcome guest at family events. She died at Sigmaringen in 1999.

Some deaths have far reaching consequences. The loss of a child is an unthinkable tragedy for any parent. Surely, the loss of Prince Ruggiero left his parents broken-hearted, as the death of any child would to a parent. However, in this case, Ruggiero's death had deeper consequences for matters of succession for, in fact, had he lived to a ripe old age and left offspring, the succession would have remained unquestioned by the family's junior branches. Ruggiero's death removed the Calabria line from the Sicilian succession. Unless the Duke of Calabria became a widower, or God forbid divorced (which he would never do), his chances of producing another son were slim. Both the Duke and his duchess were in their forties by the time their only son died, hence trying to produce another child,

without guarantee of the said child being a boy, was, well, just not part of the plan any longer. Consequently, after Calabria's death, the royal succession would pass to one of the younger branches, and this is where the Act of Cannes, signed by Carlos prior to his wedding to the Princess of Asturias, turned into a far more important document than initially expected. The succession quarrel that ensued after Calabria's death reached unimaginable levels and created a rift within the family, and their supporters, that lasted more than five decades. We will touch upon this sad episode in a forthcoming chapter. For know, suffice to say, that Ruggiero's loss was not just deeply felt by his parents and sisters, but also by the entire dynasty at large.

The Great War and its sad consequences for Germany also affected the Calabrias. Overnight, as the armies of Europe rushed in a mad dash to battle each other, multinational families like the Bourbons of the Two Sicilies were caught in the middle. The Casertas continued living in Cannes, while several of their offspring were caught behind inside the borders of both the German and Austro-Hungarian empires. The Calabrias, who continued living in Bavaria, dedicated themselves to charitable work assisting the war wounded. Ferdinando-Pio's sister, Princess Maria Immacolata and her husband, Johann Georg of Saxony, also gave themselves entirely to charitable work and providing assistance

The Duchess of Calabria holding her youngest child, Princess Urraca.

Left: The Duke and Duchess of Calabria, Princess Barbara of Bourbon-Two Sicilies and her husband Count Franz-Xaver zu Stolberg-Wernigerode.

to the Red Cross, as both were selfless humanitarians. In Austria, their brother-in-law Archduke Peter Ferdinand served in the Austro-Hungarian Army. He fought in the Russian Front and later was transferred to the Tyrol, where he fought against Italy.

The end of the war brought further challenges, particularly for the Calabrias and those family members living in post-Imperial Germany. The revolution that toppled the Kaiser and all the remaining German rulers not only did away with their political roles, but also in many instances considerably reduced their financial situation. It would take years for the succeeding republican republican regimes to settle accounts with the former ruling dynasties and for apanages to resume. And yet, once able to travel outside of Germany, the Calabrias returned to Cannes, where the Count and Countess of Caserta welcomed them with open arms after years of not setting eyes on their eldest son and his family.

The wedding procession: Princesses Maria Antonietta and Maria Cristina with Count Josef Ludwig zu Stolberg-Wernigerode. The bride and groom follow and behind them Princess Urraca and the Duke and Duchess of Calabria. Crown Prince Rupprecht of Bavaria walks behind them.

The family of the Duke of Calabria c. 1922. From left, standing: Princess Barbara (Countess zu Stolberg-Wernigerode), Count Franz-Xaver zu Stolberg-Wernigerode and Princess Maria Antonietta. Seated, in the same order: Princess Lucia, Princess Urraca, the Duchess and Duke of Calabria anf Princess Maria Cristina.

In 1922, the Duke and Duchess of Calabria presided over the wedding of their third daughter, Princess Barbara, to Count Franz-Xaver zu Stolberg-Wernigerode. The groom owned a large estate in Lower Silesia, Peterswaldau, which had been in his family's possession for generations. Franz-Xaver inherited the estate in 1905 after the early death of his father, Count Anton, who was married to Countess Elisabeth von Waldburg zu Wolfegg u. Waldsee. Interestingly, Barbara's mother-in-law was the daughter of Countess Sophie-Leopoldine von Arco-Zinneberg (1836-1909), a granddaughter of Archduchess Maria Leopoldine of Austria-Este (1776-1848), one of the daughters of Duke Ferdinando of Modena, a younger brother of Queen Maria Carolina of the Two Sicilies, Princess Barbara's own great-great-great-grandmother. Sadly, after four children born in quick succession, Princess Barbara died at Peterswaldau in January 1927, three weeks after the birth of Sophie, her last child. It is worth mentioning, perhaps, that only one of Princess Barbara's children, her eldest daughter Elisabeth (1923-2012), married and left descendants in the family of the Counts von Stillfried und Rattonitz.

The Calabrias did not have another marriage in the family until October 1938 when their daughter Princess Lucie married her distant relation the Duke of Ancona at Schloß Nymphenburg in what proved to be one of the last major gatherings of the Royal Family of the Two Sicilies before the start of the Second World War. Eugene of Savoy, Duke of Ancona, later Duke of Genoa, was the youngest child of Prince Tommaso, 2nd Duke of Genoa, and of his Bavarian-born wife, Princess Elisabeth, whose mother was Infanta Amelia of Spain, one of the daughters of Princess Luisa Carlota of the Two Sicilies, one of the daughters of King Francesco I. The groom served in the artillery and was also a senator of the kingdom of Italy. They settled in Rome where Lucie gave birth to a daughter, Isabella, in 1943. There were no other children. After the Second World War the Anconas relocated to Brazil and lived there the rest

The Duke of Calabria in later years.

of their lives. Their daughter married Alberto Frioli and with him had several children. The Friolis, along with the descendants of Princess Barbara, are the only two lines descended from the Duke and Duchess of Calabria.

On the death of his father in 1934 Prince Ferdinando, Duke of Calabria, succeeded as Head of the House, accepted without demur by the other members of the family. His death in 1960 led to a dispute about the succession that has lasted to the present day. His own preferred successor was his younger brother Ranieri, but his nephew the Infante Don Alfonso of Spain, son of Prince Carlo(s), announced that the renunciation signed by his father in 1900 was invalid and claimed the Headship of the House for himself, a claim that his son Infante Don Carlos of Spain continues to maintain.

Inseparable from this dispute is also the matter of the Grand Magistery of various orders of chivalry associated with the family, most important of which is the Sacred Military Constantinian Order of Saint George. Both sides in this dispute have impassioned supporters and finally a solution was

The wedding of the Duke of Ancona and Princess Lucia of Bourbon-Two Sicilies. The bride is surrounded by her father and by the Prince of Piedmont, future King Umberto II of Italy. To the right of the photograph is Duke Philipp Albrecht of Württemberg.

The 80th birthday of the Duchess of Calabria, Lindau, 1952. From left: The Duchess of Calabria, Crown Prince Rupprecht of Bavaria, the Duke of Calabria, Princess Wiltrud, Duchess of Urach, Princess Helmtrud of Bavaria and Princess Irmingard of Bavaria. Standing in back are: Princess Urraca, Prince Franz of Bavaria, the Duchess of Ancona, Princess Maria Cristina and Princess Maria Antonietta, Princess Gabriele of Bavaria, Princess Editha of Bavaria and Count Konstantin zu Waldburg-Zeil.

reached in early 2014, when the Duke of Noto and the Duke of Castro, representing both sides of the dispute, signed an agreement recognizing each other's claim. However, as the Duke of Castro has only two daughters, while the Duke of Noto has several sons, the conflict will sort itself out since there is no female succession in the statutes governing the former Kingdom of the Two Sicilies. It is not within the scope of this book, however, to take sides in the matter, but it would be unreasonable not to mention it. This dispute will be further discussed in the following chapter.

Princess Urraca of Bourbon-Two Sicilies.

CHAPTER VII

Carlos
Infante of Spain

T he second son, Carlo, born at Gries in the South Tyrol in 1870, and known in the family as "Nino" grew up into a personable and intelligent young man, and it was expected and hoped that he would follow the example of his elder brother and make a good match. Attempts were made to pair him off with Princess Clementine, youngest daughter of King Leopold II of the Belgians, and when this came to nothing Archduchess Elisabeth, the young daughter of the deceased Crown Prince Rudolph of Austria was also a contender.

During one of her visits to the French Riviera, Princess Clementine of Belgium had the opportunity to meet Prince Carlo, who left her with a somewhat mixed opinion. *"He is fine, very handsome. I believe him to be serious, frank and honest,"* she wrote. Furthermore, Clementine said, *"Everyone praises him. He is very pious and has all the required qualities. However, his excessive timidity makes him seem not intelligent ... I find him fine and his family are excellent, but I can hardly judge him because due to his shyness I barely spoke to him."* Prince Carlo was everything but lacking in intelligence. He was shy and did not possess the sort of personality that attracted attention or basked in making his presence felt. He was quite and shy, serious and pious, dutiful and dependable – these qualities Queen Regent Maria Cristina considered a must-have for anyone wishing to join her family. Carlo was never to disappoint her.

Prince Carlo(s) of Bourbon-Two Sicilies.

Serving as an officer in the Spanish Army, Carlo, who in Spain was known as "Carlos," was on especially good terms with the Spanish Royal Family, whose senior members at the time consisted of the Queen Regent Maria Cristina, her two daughters Infantas Maria de las Mercedes and Maria Teresa, and the young King Alfonso XIII, who was a minor. The elder daughter Mercedes was the Princess of Asturias, and had anything happened to Alfonso she would have become Queen of Spain. She and Carlos quickly became attached to each other, the relationship being regarded with a benevolent eye by the Queen Regent, who was well disposed to a Bourbon son-in-law, specially one as respected and well-liked as Carlos. Carlos and Mercedes became officially engaged in the autumn of 1900, but the announcement was not greeted with unmitigated pleasure in Spain.

The controversy over the marriage of the son of a Carlist general to the heiress presumptive to the Spanish Crown led to protests by the liberal opposition in the Cortes with demands that the Princess of Asturias or Prince Carlos renounce if the marriage was to go ahead. The terms of the marriage were agreed in formal correspondence between the Queen Regent and the Count of Caserta and this specifically excluded the need for a dynastic renunciation. The minister of Justice, in a formal statement to the Cortes, made it clear not only that a renunciation was unnecessary but also that it would not be legally binding if made. The minister gave the same advice to the Queen Regent. Nonetheless the Count was booed when he arrived in Madrid to attend the wedding and troops had to intervene to prevent unrest in the streets. The marriage ceremony took place with considerable pomp in the Royal Palace on February 14, 1901 with many foreign royals present – neither the count of Caserta nor his sons wore

Opposite page: Infante don Carlos of Spain.

The Spanish Royal Family. From left: The Princess of Asturias, King Alfonso XIII, Queen Regent Maria Cristina and Infanta María Teresa.

King Alfonso XII, father-in-law of Infante don Carlos.

their Two Sicilies decorations so as not to embarrass the Spanish government, which was on good terms with Italy.

Two months before his wedding, Prince Carlos signed a document, known as the Act of Cannes, in which he declared that he renounced his eventual rights of succession to the Throne of the Two Sicilies, in execution of the Pragmatic Decree of Charles VII and III of October 6, 1759. The necessity and the validity of this renunciation are the root cause of the ongoing dynastic dispute mentioned above.

The dispute emanated years later when Carlos' eldest son, Infante don Alfonso, laid claim to both Headship of House and to the Grand Magistery of the Constantinian Order of Saint George, one of Europe's most renowned and respected orders of chivalry. Don Alfonso's argument centered on the understanding that the Act of Cannes would have only gone into effect if his father's first wife actually inherited the throne, since the only requirement for a renunciation in Two Sicilies law was if the Crowns of Spain and the Two Sicilies were united in the same person. He, Carlos, as consort of the Queen of Spain, could not combine the Two Sicilies and Spanish crowns as per various

Opposite page: The Princess of Asturias and the Infante don Carlos, c. 1901.

A postcard sold in Spain at the time of the wedding of the Princess of Asturias and the Infante don Carlos.

previous international agreements. However, since the Princess of Asturias died in 1904, and therefore Carlos was never in any danger of being the consort of the Spanish monarch, don Alfonso considered, based on serious studies and interpretations of the documentation governing the Sicilian succession, that the Act of Cannes was therefore null and void and his rights of succession were intact and valid.

This position was questioned in 1960 by his Uncle Ranieri who Ferdinando-Pio, Duke of Calabria, had wanted to succeed as Head of the Royal House. They believed that the Act of Cannes was an explicit and immediate renunciation and that the descendants of their brother Carlo never had rights to the non-existent throne of the Two Sicilies. Equally important, was the grand mastership of the Constantinian Order, an ecclesiastical office that was bound by its own statutes, confirmed by Papal Bull and subject to canon law. This dignity had been inherited from the Farnese in 1731 and, although the administration was removed to Naples in 1768, it was still based in Parma but under the control of the King in Naples. Charles VII and III's abdication of the Two Sicilies to his son Ferdinand on 6 October 1759 did not include the Constantinian grand mastership that was renounced in a separate act ten days later. Ferdinand IV had decided to enlarge the Order's properties in the Two Sicilies and by 1797 when the French confiscated its Parmesan holdings it had become a largely Neapolitan-Sicilian institution. Ferdinand had confirmed that the crown and grand mastership were two separate dignities, each with their own laws, by a decree published in 1796. Although the Order was not mentioned in the Act of Cannes, Prince Ranieri considered the succession to the grand mastership was implied, believing it was united with the headship of the family. The Infante don Alfonso's advisers, however, believed that it was a separate dignity, as the statutes that governed it in

A photo taken after the wedding ceremony of the Princess of Asturias and the Infante don Carlos.

A wedding group photo taken at the Oriente Palace, Madrid, February 14, 1901.
Standing, from left: Princess Maria Giuseppina of Bourbon-Two Sicilies, Queen Regent Maria Cristina of Spain, the Count of Caserta, Princess Maria Pia of Bourbon-Two Sicilies, Infanta Eulalia of Spain, Infante don Carlos, Archduke Eugen of Austria, the Princess of Asturias, King Alfonso XIII, Prince Gennaro of Bourbon-Two Sicilies, the Duke of Calabria, Infamta María Teresa of Spain and the Duchess of Calabria. Seated, in the same order: Infante Isabel of Spain (Countess of Girgenti), the Countess of Caserta and Princess Carolina of Bourbon-Two Sicilies (Countess Zamoyska).

1960 required merely that the grand mastership pass by male primogeniture in the House of Bourbon as heirs of the Farnese. This in general terms are the reasons that served as the foundation for the vituperative quarrel that divided the Sicilian Royal Family for more than five decades.

The confrontation was real, and verbally violent at times, particularly among the supporters of both branches of the family claiming to the headship of house and control of the Constantinian Order. This division even affected other royal families along the continent, as many heads of house took sides and granted recognition to the claims of one of the opposing branches.

Meanwhile, don Alfonso died in 1964 and his Uncle Ranieri passed away nine years later. Both contesting claims continued alive and vibrant on the shoulders of the Duke of Calabria, Alfonso's only son, and the Duke of Castro, Ranieri's only son. In Spain, the Duke of Calabria received the unquestioned support of his uncle and cousin, the Count of Barcelona and King Juan Carlos. His father-in-law, the Count of Paris, was not as supportive of his

Queen Regent Maria Cristina of Spain.

Infante don Carlos of Spain on his wedding day to Princess Louise d'Orléans.

Infanta Luisa (Louise) of Spain.

claims and instead threw his weight behind the Castro claims.

Rapprochement between the branches began after the death of the Duke of Castro in 2008. His only son, Prince Carlo, who had used the title of Duke of Calabria, the same title styled by the Infante don Carlos, now assumed a new title, Duke of Castro, as well as a new approach to the dispute. In due time, the Duke of Castro and his Spanish-born cousin, the Duke of Noto, only son of the Infante don Carlos, reached a settlement by which they recognized each other's position, thus ending the acrimony that had besmirched the family for five decades. In 2014, while attending the beatification of Queen Maria Christina of the Two Sicilies, they both signed a document, in the presence of several family members and with that the dispute over the use of titles of the royal house came to an end with each recognizing the titles used by the other branch. Both the Infante don Carlos, Duke of Calabria and Prince Carlo, Duke of Castro, continue to maintain their claims to the headship of the royal house and that each are Constantinian Grand Masters, but of one, single Order, with parallel administrations that agree to recognize the membership of the other branch.

Now, returning to the beloved "Nino," he also assumed Spanish nationality in 1901, and a week before the wedding was elevated to the status of Infante of Spain and given the Order of the Golden Fleece.

Infante don Carlos and his wife settled down to a period of happy married bliss in the Royal Palace. Their first child, a son Alfonso, was born in November 1901, and a second son, Fernando, followed in 1903. All of the couple's children received the title of Infantes(as) of Spain in recognition of their mother's proximity to the throne. Alfonso, in fact, was his Uncle King Alfonso XIII's immediate heir from 1904 until the birth of the Prince of Asturias in 1907.

The Spanish Royal Family visiting Princess Friederike of Hannover at her home in Biarritz. Standing in back, from left: King Alfonso XIII, Baron von Pawel-Rammingen (Friederike's husband), Infante don Carlos, Infante don Fernando and Infanta doña María Teresa. Seated in the same order: Queen Victoria Eugenia, Infanta doña Luisa, Queen Mother Maria Cristina and Infanta doña Isabel (Countess of Girgenti).

By his charming manner and impeccable behavior Infante Carlos was able to overcome any opposition to him in Spain and was on excellent terms with the young King, who saw "Nino" as the brother he never had. To all intents and purposes Carlos became a Spaniard with life and soul and although devoted to his new homeland continued to maintain close relationships with his siblings and parents in Cannes.

Tragedy truck Carlos unexpectedly in 1904. His wife Mercedes, never very strong, died soon after giving birth to a little girl, Isabel Alfonsa. The death of Mercedes caused consternation within the Royal Family and leaving her grieving widower with three young children to bring up. To compound his grief, the couple's second son, Fernando, also died in August 1905. Carlos continued to carry out his military and other duties on behalf of King Alfonso XIII and also represented Spain at events abroad.

Lonely in his personal life and in need of a mother for his two

The Countess of Paris surrounded by three of her daughters. From the left: Princess Isabelle (Duchess de Guise), Princess Hélène (Duchess of Aosta) and Princess Louise (Infanta of Spain).

Infante don Carlos and his eldest son Infante don Alfonso.

surviving children, Infante Carlos was eager to marry again, and soon fixed his attentions on Princess Louise d'Orléans, youngest daughter of the Head of the French Royal House the late Count of Paris. Her mother was closely related to the Spanish Royal Family not only by title, Infanta of Spain, but also by bloodlines, as Isabelle d'Orléans was the eldest daughter of the Duke of Montpensier and the Infanta Luisa Fernanda of Spain, a sister of Queen Isabel II. Louise, who was much liked by the Spanish Royal Family, also happened to be a close relation of Carlos' as she descended from King Ferdinando I and Queen Maria Carolina several times. Queen Mother Maria Cristina, who had known Louise since birth, was also very happy that Carlos had found an excellent bride who would be equally good to her orphaned grandchildren. With great tact Carlos did not pursue the matter until King Alfonso XIII, by this time married to Princess Victoria Eugenie of Battenberg, had become father of a son and heir in 1907, but both the King and his mother Queen Maria Cristina gave the marriage their blessing.

Carlos and Louise's wedding ceremony finally took place at Woodnorton Hall in England, the home in exile of the bride's brother, the Duke d'Orléans. It was a grand affair attended by countless royals from the whole of Europe, many of whom were subsequently entertained by King Edward VII and Queen Alexandra at Windsor Castle. The wedding guests included such prominent royalty as King Alfonso XIII and Queen Victoria Eugenia of Spain, Queen Amelie of Portugal and Grand Duke Vladimir Alexandrovich and his indomitable wife Grand Duchess Marie Pavlovna the Elder. After the wedding ceremonies were concluded, Carlos and Louise returned to Spain to live, a town palace in Madrid being acquired for them. Also from this new marriage came Infante Carlos's longstanding relationship with Seville and the province of Andalucía, where his mother-in-law owned large estates. Their first child, a son named Carlos, was born in 1908, followed by three daughters: María de los "Dolores" in 1909, "María" de las Mercedes in 1910 and María de la "Esperanza" in 1914. María years later remembered her mother and described her as, *"being very worthy, but with a strong character that did not allow us to get away with much. She was very strict, but just."* The Infante Carlos, on the other hand was, *"all goodness, discretion and rectitude, sometimes he was very soft toward us. Life then was very simple and we children did not really express our opinions or demand much."* At home the children spoke Spanish with Carlos, French with their mother, Italian with their father's parents, while their nannies spoke English and German to them. Music played an important role in their education and

Infante don Carlos and Infanta doña Luisa of Spain.

Standing in back, from left: Prince Carlos, Infanta doña Isabel Alfonsa, Infante don Carlos and Infante don Alfonso. Seated, same order: Princess María de las Mercedes, Infanta doña Luisa holding Princess María de la Esperanza and Princess María de los Dolores.

from childhood, the children were frequent visitors to the palace as playmates of King Alfonso XIII's children, as well as of the children of the King's surviving sister, Infanta María Teresa, who had married her first cousin Fernando of Bavaria. Royal Decree of King Alfonso XIII granted all four children of Carlos and Luisa the style of "Royal Highness" and the same precedence and honors as those of Infantes of Spain.

Infanta doña Luisa of Spain.

With countless relations living across the continent, the children of Carlos and Luisa were raised in a cosmopolitan environment, one in which the many languages they were taught served them well. The family visited the Villa Marie Thérèse nearly every year, spending time at the seaside resort of La Napoule. They also traveled to Poland and Czechoslovakia, as well as Austria, Italy, Germany and Switzerland. They visited Orléans relatives at the Château d'Eu in Normandy, as well as the Manoir d'Anjou in Belgium, where Infanta Luisa's brother-in-law the Duke de Guise kept a court in exile since he was banned from entering, much less living, in France. María, later Countess of Barcelona, always remembered fondly these visits and the happy times spent surrounded by the extended family, particularly the gatherings in Cannes under the loving care of their Caserta grandparents.

After the death of Louise's mother in 1919, she inherited the Palace of Villamanrique near Seville, which was to become the couple's second

Silver Wedding anniversary of Infante don Carlos and Infanta doña Luisa of Spain. (1932)

Count Jan-Kanty Zamoyski.

home. Louise's mother, the Countess of Paris, was the eldest child of the Infanta Luisa Fernanda, a sister of Queen Isabel II, and of her ambitious, and at times meddlesome, French husband, Prince Antoine of Orléans, Duke of Montpensier. He amassed a phenomenal fortune during his years in Spain. His holdings, besides vast investments, also included large estates in Andalucía. Some of these landed estates, in fact, remain in the hands of several of Montpensier's descendants.

Interestingly, in 1921 the Infante don Carlos was put forward as a candidate for the Hungarian throne. Documentation to back this previously unknown fact is found in the archives of the royal palace – his candidature was supported by Spain, needless to say, France and Great Britain, but the plan came to nothing because Horthy did not want a king to replace him.

By then, Infante Carlos had achieved an extremely commendable career in Spain's military. For many years her served in the famed Princess's Hussars, one of the Spanish Royal army's most prestigious regiments. He also continued his close friendship with King Alfonso XIII, who did not begrudge Carlos for rebuilding his life after the tragic loss of the Princess of Asturias. The Infante, in fact, was one of the most prominent men from the inner

The family of the Infante Carlos and Infanta Luisa were deeply Catholic. This image, taken by the side of a road, shows Luisa with her daughters during a "romería," a pilgrimage to a holy site. Standing in back, from left: Infanta Isabel Alfonsa and Infanta Luisa. Seated, same order: Princesses María, Dolores and Esperanza.

circle of the Spanish monarch, who trusted Carlos implicitly and whose loyalty was unquestioned. It was because of his trust in Carlos that King Alfonso XIII appointed him Governor General of Andalucía, a position that required, to the family's absolute delight, that Carlos relocate to Seville. From there, Carlos and his family had easy access to Luisa's estate at Villamanrique, some 25 miles from Seville.

In 1929 Carlos and Luisa presided over the wedding festivities for his daughter Infanta Isabel Alfonsa. That same year the couple traveled to Barcelona to visit the Universal Exposition. The following year, King Alfonso XIII appointed Infante Carlos as Governor General of Catalonia, forcing the family to depart from their beloved Seville and start a new chapter in Barcelona. Due to Carlos' unquestioned service and great expertise in military matters, King Alfonso XIII also

Infanta Isabel Alfonsa of Spain.

The wedding of the Count and Countess of Paris, Palermo, April 1931. From the front: Grand Duchess Marie Georgievna of Russia with Prince Pedro Henrique d'Orléans-Bragançã; Princess René of Bourbon-Parma with Prince Paul of Greece; the Duke and Duchess of Puglie; Princess Dolores of Bourbon-Two Sicilies and the Duke of Spoleto; Princess Esperanza of Bourbon-Two Sicilies and the Duke of Ancona (obscured); Princess Teresa d'Orléans-Bragança with Prince Christopher of Greece; and behind them is Prince Philipp of Hesse.

Princess Dolores of Bourbon-Two Sicilies.

appointed him Inspector General of the Army. He was still serving in these two important posts when the monarchy suddenly fell.

When the Spanish Republic was declared in 1931, Infante Carlos and his family followed King Alfonso XIII into exile and settled in Paris. The Infante and his family had just returned from Palermo, Sicily, where they attended the wedding ceremony of the Count of Paris, Henri, and of his beautiful bride Isabelle, eldest daughter of Prince Pedro d'Alcantara, Prince of Grão Pará, himself the eldest son of the Princess Imperial of Brazil and her French husband the Count d'Eu.

Exile proved a difficult time for the Infante Carlos and his family. With the Infante's army career at an end and cut off from their possessions, there began a period of great uncertainty for the family. They continued to make regular visits to Cannes until the death of the Count of Caserta in 1934 and also spent extended periods with their many relatives in Poland, Austria and Germany as well as with King Alfonso XIII, who in exile had settled in Rome.

In the meantime the children had started to marry. The first to leave the family home was Infanta Isabel Alfonsa, who married Polish Count Jan Zamoyski in 1929. They had met at Uncle Ranieri's wedding, and he was the brother of Ranieri's wife Carolina – their mother a sister of the Countess of Caserta. In 1935 Princess María married her cousin the Infante Juan of Spain, Prince of Asturias (who later used the title of Count of Barcelona) and became the mother of King Juan Carlos of Spain. The following year her half-brother Alfonso, the elder son of Infante Carlos, married in Vienna his second cousin Princess Alicia of Bourbon-Parma. She was the daughter of Duke Elias of Parma and of his Austrian wife, Archduchess Maria Anna, one of the many daughters of Archduke Friedrich of Austria, Duke of Teschen, eldest brother of former Queen Regent Maria Cristina of Spain. Princess Alicia, like her husband, was also a descendant of the Sicilian Royal Family since her paternal grandmother, Duchess Maria Pia of Parma, was born a Princess of the Two Sicilies, as well as being a sister of the Count of Caserta, Infante don Alfonso's grandfather. It was Alfonso, who had challenged the claim of his uncle, Prince Ranieri, to succeed as head of the house, a position maintained by his son Infante Carlos to this day.

Prince Carlos of Bourbon-Two Sicilies.

In 1936 the Spanish Civil War broke out and the young Prince Carlos immediately decided to sign up on the Nationalist side. He had been studying engineering and was also a talented sculptor. His family expected that Carlos would marry Princess Teresa d'Orléans-Bragança, the youngest child of the Prince of Grão Pará and his Bohemian-born wife, Countess Elisabeth Dobrzensky von Dobrzenicz. In September 1936, to everyone's deep sorrow, Carlos was killed in action at Elgoibar. His early death was a grave loss to the family as Carlos was much-liked and beloved by all the extended cousinhood. Princess Teresa remained unattached until 1957 when she married a Portuguese gentleman, Ernesto Martorell.

In 1937, a year after her brother's death, Princess Dolores married her third cousin, the extremely wealthy Polish Prince Josef-August Czartoryski and went to live on his vast estates. The Czartoryskis also owned a famed and elegant Parisian residence, the Hôtel Lambert, site of many family events and gatherings. Josef-August was the son of Prince Adam Czartoryski, Duke of Klewan and Zukow (1872-1937), who was the son of Princess Marguerite of Orléans (1846-1893), who was a first cousin of the Infanta Louise, Dolores's mother.

The Infante Carlos and his family, toward the end of his life. From left: Princess Esperanza, Infante Alfonso, Infanta Luisa, Infante Carlos, Infanta Isabel Alfonsa, the Countess of Barcelona and Princess Dolores.

After this wedding, with most of his children wonderfully married, the Infante Carlos, then almost seventy years old, decided to return to Spain. The Civil War had ended and the Nationalists won the conflict. Spain, under the rule of General Franco, was pacified and the long period of reconciliation and reconstruction could then begin in earnest. The family settled in the famed Palace of Villamanrique, an estate near Seville, his wife's property inherited from her mother and originally belonging to the Duke de Montpensier. Princess Esperanza, in fact, inherited Villamanrique, and when not living at her husband's properties in Petropolis, Brazil, she called Villamanrique home.

The Second World War caused further devastation to the family. Princess Dolores and her husband arrived from Poland in 1944 as refugees, having lost their entire possessions following the Soviet occupation of that country. The Zamoyskis also lost everything, as did the Saxony royal family. One happy event in this period of turmoil was the wedding of the youngest daughter Princess Esperanza to Prince Pedro Gastão d'Orléans-Bragança. It was celebrated in Seville in 1944 and attended by a healthy number of royalties, particularly given the difficult times Europe was living under. It was to be the Infante Carlos' last joy.

Infanta Isabel Alfonsa of Spain and Count Jan-Kanty Zamoyski.

A gathering of royal cousins in Andalucía. From left: Prince Pedro Gastão d'Orléans-Bragança, Infanta Isabel Alfonsa of Spain, Prince Peter of Schleswig-Holstein, Infanta Beatrice of Spain, Princess Esperanza d'Orléans-Bragança, Princess Marie Alix of Schleswig-Holstein, unidentified, Princess Alexandra of Hohenlohe-Langenburg and Princess Beatrice of Orléans-Borbón.

Infante Carlos lived on until 1949, dying peacefully at his home in Andalucía in November 1949. His wife followed him in 1958 and both are buried, along with their son Carlos, in the Church of El Salvador in Seville. Their many descendants, scattered throughout Europe and Brazil, share fond memories of them, and it would no doubt be a source of intense satisfaction to Infante Carlos to see the Monarchy in Spain restored so successfully in the person of his grandson King Juan Carlos and now continued on the shoulders of his great-grandson King Felipe VI.

If anything proves that being born royal is no guarantee that a happy life is in store, one only needs to look at the children of the Infante don Carlos. Their life began inside palaces and theirs was a pristine existence that included loving parents, servants, excellent instructors and tutors, as well as travel and access to a lifestyle enjoyed by only the very few. That however, did not translate into happy marriages or isolation from tragedy and suffering.

As we mentioned before, the first of the children to marry was Infanta Isabel Alfonsa. The wedding was marred by the death of her grandmother just a few days before it was scheduled to take place. The Queen Mother, not wishing

Infanta Isabel Alfonsa in later years.

Princess María of Bourbon-Two Sicilies.

to disrupt her granddaughter's special day, requested that the wedding festivities proceed unaltered. Isabel Alfonsa, who remains unknown to most readers, was a simple and uncomplicated woman. She was the one who began calling King Alfonso XIII, "Tío Rey," (Uncle King) a sobriquet later adopted by all the children of his family, including Infante don Carlos' second family. She shied away from pomp and circumstance and instead dedicated her time to two of her favorite passions, animals and gardening. However, being the heir to her mother's considerable inheritance, whoever married Isabel Alfonsa, stood to gain access to her fortune.

Count Jan-Kanty Zamoyski, called "Jas" by the family, was one of the countless children of Princess Carolina of Bourbon-Two Sicilies, the only surviving sibling of the Countess of Caserta. Jas Zamoyski, therefore, was a first cousin of the Infante don Carlos, his father-in-law. He was born in Cracow in 1900 as the eighth child of his mother and her Polish husband, Count Andrzej Zamoyski (1852-1927). Difficulties between the young couple began soon after settling in Hungary, where their two eldest children were born, Karol and Maria Cristina. Her sister, María, later recalled that Jas was a charming man who enjoyed entertaining and having a fun time, but who also drank far too much, this weakness being the cause of the couple's disagreements. Still, two further children were born to the couple, Jozef and Maria Teresa, in 1935 and 1938 respectively. Further complicating their troubles was Jas's decision to invest most of his fortune, and a sizable share of his wife's, in a business venture that collapsed. When the war began in 1939, any chance of success for the business evaporated. Isabel Alfonsa left Eastern Europe and reached the relative safety and quiet of Andalucía, while Jas settled in Cannes. The family assisted in whatever way they could and Isabel Alfonsa was bought a farm to exploit so she could front the needs of her four children. This suited her perfectly and she quickly abandoned any trappings of royalty that she might have still had. It was not uncommon to see her driving a jeep into Seville where she sold milk and produce. *"Learn from the Infanta,"* common folk would say while acknowledging her greeting, *"look at what the Infanta does to raise her children!"* When family and friends tried to get Isabel Alfonsa to change her ways, she would simply reply, *"I am who I am and if someone doesn't like it, I don't care."*

Isabel Alfonsa of Spain died in 1985, surviving her estranged husband by nearly a quarter of a century. Sadly, she lived through the death of two of her children: Karol died in Seville in October 1979, two days short of his forty-ninth birthday; while Maria Cristina had died in 1959. Countess Maria Teresa, who always exhibited deep piety, joined the Carmelite nuns in Madrid. Both Isabel Alfonsa's sons, Karol and Jozef, married and had children.

Infante don Juan of Spain at the Royal Naval Academy.

The Prince and Princess of Asturias, Juan and María, stopped in the United States during their honeymoon. The couple traveled for six months and went around the world.

Princess María, a woman of unimaginable character and integrity, was the next of the Infante Carlos' children to marry. In exile, María had lived with her parents who remained close to King Alfonso XIII. Uncle King had initially arrived in France after the fall of the monarchy, but eventually settled in Rome. Queen Victoria Eugenia, after a lifetime of having to live with a husband who was, well, most disrespectful to their marriage, settled in Lausanne, Switzerland. Also, during exile, Uncle King had suffered greatly on a personal level. His eldest son, the Prince of Asturias, a hemophiliac, became estranged from his father when he decided to marry a lady of Cuban extraction and lacking in the necessary quarterings to become a member of the Spanish Royal family. Marrying against his father's will cost Asturias his place in the line of succession. Then Uncle King convinced his next son, Infante Jaime, to renounce his rights since he was deft and that curtailed his ability to communicate. In his stead, the came Infante Juan, the sailor third son of the king. A further tragedy affecting the family happened in 1934 when Infante Gonzalo, Uncle King's fourth son,

The Silver Wedding Anniversary of the Counts of Barcelona, Estoril, 1960. Clockwise from top: the Count of Barcelona, the Prince of Asturias, the Countess of Barcelona, Infanta Margarita and Infanta Pilar.

The Countess of Barcelona.

The Prince of Asturias and Princess Sophie of Greece during their wedding ceremony, Athens, May 14, 1962.

also a hemophiliac, died as a consequence of minor injuries suffered in an automobile while on vacation in Austria. Therefore, by 1935, with Infante Juan, now Prince of Asturias, the only son with succession rights, his marriage became a matter of the utmost importance. Enter María!

Don Juan had tried to get Princess Maria of Savoy, youngest child of King Vittorio Emanuele III to accept his approaches. The young princess was not interested in wearing a crown, even an exiled one, and she treated Juan with coolness. Annoyed, the young man continued his search and soon enough he set his sights on the very dependable and dutiful cousin María, Who Uncle King called "la Brava," (the upset), as she had little tolerance for nonsense. Juan and María talked, they found that between them they could make a marriage work and soon after became engaged. Their multitudinous wedding was celebrated in Rome on October 12, 1935. The festivities were attended by countless royal relations as well as thousands of Spaniards who traveled to the Italian capital to witness a marriage that was going to play a very important role in the future of the dynasty and the eventual restoration of the monarchy in 1975.

After their honeymoon, which took them from Europe to America to Asia, the Middle East and back to Europe, Juan and María, who would be later known as Count and Countess of Barcelona, settled in Cannes. While there, María gave birth to a daughter, Infanta María del Pilar. In 1938 a son, Juan Carlos, was born in Rome, where two more children (Margarita and Alfonso) were born in 1939 and 1941 respectively. Eventually, the Count of Barcelona moved his family to Estoril, a picturesque seaside resort in the outskirts of Lisbon, Portugal. Soon enough other extended family members settled in Portugal as well, including the Count and Countess of Paris (and their endless troop of children), King Umberto II of Italy, King Carol II of Romania, Queen Mother Giovanna of Bulgaria (with her children Simeon II and Marie Louise), the Dukes of Bragança and Archduke Joseph of Austria and his equally large troop of rowdy children.

The Countess of Barcelona was already living in Estoril when news of her father's worsening health arrived. The Spanish government put roadblocks that prevented María to be by the Infante Carlos's bedside as he expired. She never forgave General Franco for what she believed was a vicious decision that kept her from saying a final goodbye to her father. In 1958, when news of her mother's worrisome state arrived, María simply got in a car and drove into Spain. No border guard dared stop her entry into Spain. By then, she had already experienced the untold pain involved in the loss of a child when her youngest son Alfonso was killed while he and Infante Juan Carlos played with a gun owned by their father. It was a blow from which María Barcelona never recovered.

Life in exile was, at times, extremely difficult. The Count of Barcelona felt despondent by his inability to outsmart Franco into restoring the monarchy on him. These frustrations and others led the couple to lived through some very difficult times. In the end, however, they both worked at changing course and their relationship was not only restored, but also remained solid and lasting. Further pressure on

King Juan Carlos I and Queen Sofía with their children: the Prince of Asturias (Felipe VI), Infanta Elena and Infanta Cristina.

the couple was placed by the departure of their daughters: in 1967 Infanta Pilar married don Luis Gómez-Acebo y de Estrada, a Spanish aristocrat; in 1972 Infanta Margarita married Dr. Carlos Zurita. Both daughters, given ducal titles by their father, Badajoz and Soria respectively, eventually settled in Madrid, where they raised their families.

When General Franco chose Infante Juan Carlos, who in 1962 had married Princess Sophie of Greece, to succeed him with the title of "King," the Count of Barcelona felt betrayed. Relations between him and Juan Carlos reached a low ebb and it was María who played an instrumental role in bridging the rift between father and son. Hence, when General Franco died in November 1975, King Juan Carlos I began his reign. Many of his critics referred to him as *"Juan Carlos the brief,"* because they believed he would not last. Not only did he prove them wrong, but King Juan Carlos navigated Spain through the treacherous waters toward democracy.

Peace within the family was finally reached when the Count of Barcelona "abdicated" his historic rights on King

The Count and Countess of Barcelona in old age.

Juan Carlos. Son after that, Juan and María relocated to Madrid where they would live the remaining years of their life. Once established in the Spanish capital, the Count and Countess of Barcelona led very private lives. Doña María supported several charities, while don Juan regfrained from political activity. Above all, both wanted their son the King to succeed in establishing a monarchical system with deep roots.

The Count of Barcelona, a jovial man with a large presence, died in in 1993. His wife survived him until January 1, 2000. She died in Lanzarote, the Canary Islands. She had traveled there just days before to welcome the new century surrounded by her family. Behind, María, Countess of Barcelona, left an unquestioned reputation as perhaps one of the most revered and respected princesses to ever come from the Neapolitan Bourbons.

Although we will discuss him shortly, the next one to marry was Infante don Alfonso, who married in Vienna in April 1936. Had Prince Carlos of Bourbon-Two Sicilies not fallen during the Spanish civil war, it is quite likely that he would have been the next of the Infante Carlos's children to marry. However, that was not to be and instead the next one to settle down was Princess María de los Dolores. She married in Lausanne, Switzerland, in August 1937. The groom was Prince Josef-August Czartoryski, born in Warsaw in 1907. He was the eldest son among seven children from the family created by Prince Adam Czartoryski and his wife the former Countess Maria-Ludovika Krasinska. María Barcelona described her brother-in-law as *"enchanting."* Josef-August was no stranger to the Sicilian extended family since his eldest sister, Malgorzata, had married Prince Gabriele of Bourbon-Two Sicilies in 1927. Furthermore, the Czartoryski siblings were the grandchildren of Princess Marguerite d'Orléans (1846-1893), a daughter of the Duke de Nemours and hence granddaughter of Princess Marie-Amélie of the Two Sicilies, one of the daughters of King Ferdinando I and Queen Maria Carolina.

Dolores and her husband initially settled in Poland, where his vast estates were located. However, the start of the

The wedding of Princess Dolores of Bourbon-Two Sicilies and Prince Josef-Auguste Czartorysli. Seated, from the left: King Alfsonso XIII of Spain, Queen Amelie of Portugal, King Ferdinand of Bulgaria, the newlyweds, Infante Carlos, Infanta Luis and the Countess of Barcelona.

Second World War and Nazi Germany's invasion of that country, forced the Czartoryskis to depart for the safety provided by Andalucía. They never expected that they would never again set eyes on the land of Josef-Auguste's birth. In 1940 Dolores gave birth to their first son, Adam Karol. The birthing took place in Seville, where the Czartoryskis lived with Infante Carlos and Infanta Luisa. They were still there when news reached them that Prince Ludwik, Josef-August's youngest brother, was killed in action. Already deeply depressed by the probable loss of his Polish properties, Josef-Auguste seemed to have lost hope. Attending his sister-in-law Esperanza's wedding late that same year, also failed to lift the somber clouds consuming every breath of energy. In the midst of these difficult times, Dolores gave birth to a second son, Ludwik, in March 1945. He was named in memory of his late uncle, but the baby was destined to have a short life and died in May 1946. Despondent and exhausted Prince Josef-August lost the will to live; he died six weeks later. He was but thirty-eight years of age.

Widowed and with an infant child, having lost most of her possessions in Poland, Dolores remained in

Princess Dolores and her sister the Countess of Barcelona.

Athens, 1962: Princess Dolores and her second husband Carlos Chias Osorio.

Seville as she rebuilt her life. A further blow to her spirits was provided by the loss of her father in 1949. However, the following year, she surprised the family when marrying Mr. Carlos Chias Osorio, a young man sixteen years her junior, who had been hired as tutor to her son. Perhaps her family took pity on how much suffering poor Dolores had experienced and they were more than hopeful that this new marriage would bring her much needed happiness. In her memoirs, María Barcelona mentioned her brother-in-law Carlos saying that, "*I love him very much.*" Carlos and Dolores did not have any children. Their marriage lasted until her death in 1996.

Princess Esperanza, the family's youngest child, was also the last one to marry. For years she had been in love with Prince Pedro Gastão d'Orléans-Bragança, brother of the beautiful Isabelle, Countess of Paris. He was born at the Château d'Eu, the country estate owned by his paternal grandparents, Gaston d'Eu and Princess Imperial Isabel of Brazil, a granddaughter of King Francesco I of the Two Sicilies. Pedro Gastão was a dashing and debonair young man with an infectious and irresistible personality, character traits that he retained throughout his long life. He had spent his youth between Eu and Paris, as well as long visits to Brazil, where his family owned large estates, mainly in and around the Imperial city of Petropolis, where the family lived in one of the Imperial palaces. The start of the Second World War had delayed Pedro Gastão and Esperanza from making official what everyone expected. They finally married in Seville on December 18, 1944. Their wedding was attended by a bevy of royalty, among them the Count and Countess of Paris with some of their children), Prince Alvaro of Orléans-Borbón and his wife Princess Carla, Prince Ataúlfo of Orléans-Borbón, as well as the Czartoryskis, Infante Carlos and Infanta Luisa, Infante Alfonso and Infanta Alicia, Princess Pedro d'Alcantara and her daughter Teresa (the Groom's mother and sister), and Infante Luis Alfonso (eldest son of Ferdinand of Bavaria and María Teresa of Spain), among others.

Soon after their wedding, Pedro Gastão and Esperanza settled in Brazil, where in the fall of 1945 she gave birth in Rio de Janeiro to their first child, Pedro de Alcântara. In due course five other children (Maria da Glória, Afonso, Manoel, Cristina and Francisco) joined the family. These five offspring were born in Petropolis. After her mother's death, Esperanza inherited the estate at Villamanrique, the third woman in her family to so since 1891. Princess Esperanza also remained very close to her sisters and

Prince Carlos and Princess Esperanza of Bourbon-Two Sicilies.

The wedding of Princess Esperanza of Bourbon-Two Sicilies and Prince Pedro Gastão d'Orléans-Bragança. From the left: Infanta Alicia, Infante Carlos, Princess Teresa d'Orléans-Bragança, Princess Pedro d'Alcantara d'Orléans-Bragança, the newlyweds, the Countess of Paris, Infanta Luisa, Princess Dolores Czartoryska, Princess Carla de Orléans-Borbón, Prince Josef-August Czartoryski and Infante José Eugemnio of Spain.

was an adored aunt of King Juan Carlos. In fact, in She continued dividing her time between Andalucía and Brazil, dying in Villamanrique in August 2005. Pedro Gastão survived his beloved wife four years and passed away in November 2009.

Of their children only Maria da Glória made a dynastic marriage. She married at Villamanrique Crown Prince Alexander of Yugoslavia, only child of King Peter II and Queen Alexandra, née Greece, a first cousin of Queen Sofía, consort of former King Juan Carlos of Spain. Alexander and Maria da Glória had three sons (Peter, Philip and Alexander) before divorcing in 1985. That same year she married don Ignacio de Medina y Fernández de Córdoba, Duke of Segorbe, the youngest child of the Duchess of Medinaceli, the premier peer of Spain. The Segorbes have two daughters, Sol and Luna de Medina y Orléans-Bragança.

Now, before concluding this chapter, let us discuss briefly the life of Infante don Alfonso, the firstborn son of Infante Carlos and the Princess of Asturias. He was born in Madrid on November 30, 1901. Between 1904 and 1907, as previously mentioned, he was heir presumptive of King Alfonso XIII, his uncle. In due time, Alfonso entered the army and continued his studies. As the heir to his mother's large inheritance, he was considerably wealthy. When the republic was proclaimed, Alfonso

Princess Esperanza of Bourbon-Two Sicilies.

Infante Alfonso of Spain. left Spain and lived abroad for the next few years. A physical ailment prevented him to fight during the Civil War.

Infante Alfonso married a close relation, Princess Alicia of Bourbon-Parma (b. 1917). She was one of the daughters of Prince Elias and of his Habsburg wife, Archduchess Maria Anna. Elias, as the son of Princess Maria Pia of Bourbon-Two Sicilies was a grandson of King Ferdinando II of the Two Sicilies, Infante Alfonso's great-grandfather. Alicia's mother was also closely related to the Sicilians since she was the daughter of Archduke Friedrich of Austria, Duke of Teschen, a nephew of Queen Maria Theresa of the Two Sicilies, Ferdinando II's consort. The couple's wedding was celebrated in Vienna in April 1936 and within a year Alicia gave birth to their first child, a daughter named Teresa. The following year, Infanta Alicia gave birth to their second child, a son named Carlos, who was born in Lausanne, Switzerland. Two years later Alfonso and Alicia had a third child, Inés, who was to be the family's last baby.

In due course, Infante Alfonso returned to Spain and became involved in the reconstruction effort that the

Princess Alicia of Bourbon-Parma.

Elias and Maria Anna of Bourbon-Parma.

The wedding of Infante Alfonso of Spain and Princess Alicia of Bourbon-Parma. From left: Infante Carlos, Prince Elias of Bourbon-Parma, Infanta María Cristina of Spain, Princess Maria Cristina of Bourbon-Parma, Archduchess Maria Anna, King Alfonso XIII, the newlyweds and Infanta Luisa of Spain.

country was undergoing. The civil war was devastating, Spain was in ruins and everyone's fortunes had suffered greatly during the conflict and the difficult first years of the Franco regime. Alfonso and Alicia had a home in Madrid and also a beautiful estate, La Toledana. Rebuilding took years of effort, but neither the Infante nor his wife shied away from the sacrifices required by this task. In the meantime, the children were sent to school and Alfonso remained in close contact with his cousin and brother-in-law the Count of Barcelona. In fact, when Infante Juan Carlos, by then recognized by monarchists as Prince of Asturias, was brought to be educated in Spain, his cousin Carlos was one of the youngsters chosen to join the small school Franco and the Count of Barcelona organized for the future King of Spain. Juan Carlos and his first cousin Carlos developed a close relationship during those bygone days and that relationship has remained intact and steadfast until today. This bond of friendship, truly approaching brotherhood, is perhaps one of the reasons behind King Juan Carlos elevating his cousin to the rank of Infante of Spain in 1994. These close family links have continued

The Countess of Paris and Infante Alfonso of Spain.

The family of Infante Alfonso and Infanta Alicia. From left: Princess Inés, Princess Teresa, Infanta Alicia, Infante Alfonso and Prince Carlos.

between the children of both couples, Juan Carlos and Sofía, Carlos and Anne.

In 1949, after his father's death, Infante Alfonso notified his Uncle Calabria that he believed that the Act of Cannes was invalid and did not apply to his branch. This decision to reivindicate his dynastic rights to the succession to the inexistent throne of the Two Sicilies ignited the rift that was to consume untold energy between the descendants of the Count of Caserta. Infante Alfonso also but a stop to a stipend his father had always paid to his brother Prince Ranieri, whose finances had always bordered on the precarious, as they were for most members of the Sicilian dynasty. Remember that the Savoys disposed them and the few properties left to them from the Farnese inheritance had long been sold off. The Duke of Calabria incensed by his nephew's decision, never replied to Infante Alfonso's letter announcing his plans to him. Uncle Ranieri, whom Calabria wished to succeed both as Head of House and Grand Master of the Constantinian Order of St. George, was quite displeased with his nephew as well.

A further complication took place in January 1960. Soon after the death of the Duke of Calabria, Infante Alfonso announced that he was the Head of House Two Sicilies.

Infante Alfonso and Infanta Alicia.

Princess Teresa and the Marqués de Laula with four of their children: Rodrigo, Alicia, Alfonso and baby Beatriz Moreno y de Borbón. (1967)

Princess Inés and don Luis de Morales with the Duke of Calabria.

Uncle Ranieri also laid claim to the position. Both sides also claimed to be the Grand Masters of the Constantinian Order of St. George. Consequently, the dynasty's supporters and members of the Order found themselves supporting either side. This same fate affected various Heads of House across Europe: the Count of Barcelona, and later King Juan Carlos, supported Infantes Alfonso and Carlos, while others, among them most prominently the Count of Paris, supported and recognized Uncle Ranieri. It was a right royal mess, one that remained simmering and open for far too long and was not solved until 2014.

In 1964, Infante Alfonso attended the Athens wedding of his nephew the Prince of Asturias to Princess Sophie (Sofía) of Greece, eldest child of King Paul and Queen Frederica of the Hellenes. Along with him were his half sisters (Dolores and Esperanza); all in Athens to participate in what became the most regal wedding witnessed by Europe in the 1960s. However, to all present it became clear that don Alfonso was not himself. He seemed to have aged prematurely and his physical condition was the source of considerable concern. It was the last time that the public at large would see this relatively unknown man who at one point was kept from the Spanish throne by the heartbeat of his Uncle King. Infante Alfonso died in Vienna in February 1964. His widow, Infanta doña Alicia, continues living in Spain and she is two years from celebrating her centennial.

Alfonso and Alicia's daughters married quietly, without any pomp and circumstance in fact. Princess Teresa married in Madrid in 1961 don Íñigo Moreno y Arteaga, 12th Marquis de Laula (a title he held until 2010, when a lawsuit presented a decade earlier by the Duke of Infantado, a cousin, deprived Íñigo of his title – luckily King Juan Carlos compensated his cousin's husband by granting him the title of Marques de Laserna), scion of several prominent Spanish aristocratic families. The Laulas had seven children, although only six survive.

The year following Infante don Alfonso's death, his son presided over the wedding of Princess Inés to don Luis de Morales y Aguado. This marriage did not last long and after four children Princess Inés and her husband divorced. Both Princess Teresa and her sister Princess Inés live in Spain.

Upon his father's disappearance, Carlos of Bourbon-Two Sicilies claimed the title of Duke of

The Duke and Duchess of Calabria on their wedding day. Behind them are the Infanta Alicia and the Count of Paris, followed by the Countess of Paris and the Count de Clermont.

Calabria as Head of the Sicilian Royal House. His decision did not set well with Uncle Ranieri or his son Prince Ferdinando. It was also not supported by a number of other Heads of House, among them the Count of Paris, who had also opposed the late Infante Alfonso. By then the differences between Carlos and the Count of Paris involved more than the Sicilian succession.

Princess Anne of France was one of the guests at the wedding of Princess Teresa and then Marqués de Laula. It seems that from that day onward Carlos and Anne decided to build a life together. Anne was at one time rumored to be a possible bride for King Simeon II, but nothing came of that. Anyhow, uniting Carlos and Anne, besides close family links, was their friendship with the Prince of Asturias, Juan Carlos, also present at his cousin Teresa's wedding. The following year, during the wedding in Athens, Carlos and Anne, who were among the guests, seemed to be inseparable. Anne was later invited to spend time at la Toledana and by then it was expected that the announcement of her engagement to Carlos was just a matter of time. Several French historians, as well as a number of journalists, have argued that the

Count of Paris, who was rather vocal in his opposition to the Infante's claims to headship of house, disrupted the wedding plans. This situation was further complicated when Carlos confirmed his father's position and announced his own succession to headship of house in 1964. The Count of Paris, siding with the remaining princes of Bourbon-Two Sicilies, refused Carlos recognition of his claims.

With both Carlos and the Count of Paris refusing to budge an inch, the engagement was tabled for the time being. To further his banking and legal career, Carlos left Europe and lived in America for a year. While away he interned for several prestigious entities, like the Chase Manhattan Bank in New York City. Meanwhile, Princess Anne remained in Europe and waited for fate to help her destiny. The couple's patience and tenacity paid off and in late 1964 her father relented and agreed to Anne's wedding. This

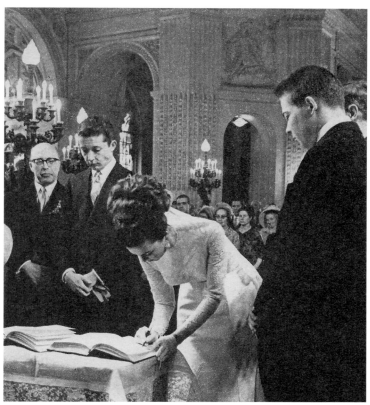

The wedding ceremony of the Duke and Duchess of Calabria. From left: Duke Roberto II of Parma, the Duke and Duchess of Calabria, and Prince Michel of France – Dreux, May 1965.

The Duke of Calabria and his mother Infanta Alicia.

The Duke and Duchess of Calabria at home.

The arrival of the Duke of Noto. Standing in back: the Duke and Duchess of Calabria, the Countess of Paris.
At front: Princess Cristina, Princess Maria, Infanta Alicia holding baby Pedro, Duke of Noto.

The Duke and Duchess of Calabria.

The Duke and Duchess of Calabria and the Duke of Noto.

The Duke and Duchess of Calabria in formal attire.

same tenacity, the Infante and his wife have demonstrated in building a pristine reputation, all while dedicating themselves with true abnegation to their children and their many responsibilities. Whether serving their cousin King Juan Carlos, raising their exquisitely educated children or leading discrete lives dedicated to work, charity and duty, Carlos and Anne succeeded in becoming an examplary couple.

Curiously, those invited to the wedding ceremony at Dreux in May 1965, found themselves witnesses to a peculiar circumstance. Keeping his opposition to Carlos's Sicilian claims, the Count of Paris' invitation to his daughter's wedding announced Anne was marrying *"HRH Prince Carlos of Bourbon."* The groom, not to be outdone, sent out invitations announcing, *"the wedding of HRH the Duke of Calabria to HRH Princess Anne of France."* One French journalist mischievously recalled that, *"it was as if the bride was marrying, on the same day, two different gentlemen."* The issue of what orders would be worn by guests was resolved when Carlos and his father-in-law agreed that to avoid confrontations: gentlemen would wear suits, not uniforms or decorations. There was

The Duke and Duchess of Calabria at home.

also no large wedding banquet. Instead, both families and the most important guests were treated to a family lunch at the Coeur Volant, the residence of the Counts of Paris. In the end it all went off without a hitch. It is worth noting, however, that besides wearing a beautiful diamond tiara worn by several princesses of her dynasty, Princess Anne also, on her wedding day, wore earrings inherited through various generations from Queen Maria Carolina, an ancestor of groom and bride many times over.

The Duke and Duchess of Calabria settled in a large apartment in Madrid and frequently resided at La Toledana, the large estate Carlos inherited from his father. Located some eighty miles from Madrid, La Toledana is an estate measuring several thousand hectares composed of arable land and a hunting reserve, a sport the Duke of Calabria has always enjoyed, much like everyone else in his extended family. The estate has also witnessed several large family gatherings, among them the weddings of Princesses Cristina and Maria, the Calabrias' eldest daughters, with members of the Spanish Royal Family among the guests.

Nearly a year after their wedding, Carlos and Anne had their first child, a daughter, Cristina. Her birth took place in Madrid, where the Duchess of Calabria would give birth to all the couple's children. In April 1967, thirteen months after

Standing in back, from the left: Princess María, the Duke of Calabria, the Duke of Noto and Princess Inés. Seated, same order: Princess Cristina, the Duchess of Calabria and Princess Victoria.

Cristina's birth, the Calabrias had a second daughter, Maria. The following year saw the birth of the couple's first, and only son, Pedro, who received the title of Duke of Noto. Three years later, a fourth child was born, Inés. Finally in 1976, the Duchess of Calabria gave birth to their last child, Victoria.

Meanwhile, the Duke of Calabria built a brilliant career as a lawyer specialized in financial and banking affairs, while also founding several very successful enterprises. He also served as president of various associations dealing with the nobility and the defense of nature, among others. His absolute discretion has earned him the trust of his cousin King Juan Carlos, whose father also thought the world of the Duke of Calabria. At the same time, the Duke of Calabria, who since 1994 is an Infante of Spain, as mentioned before, has served as Grand Master of the Constantinian Order of St. George.

The first of the Calabria children to marry was Princess Cristina. Her wedding to Mr. Pedro López-Quesada, scion of an important banking family, was celebrated at La Toledana in July 1994. Two years later Princess Maria married, also at

La Toledana, her distant cousin Archduke Simeon of Austria, one of the grandsons of Emperor Karl and Empress Zita. Interestingly, Simeon and Maria's children are descended from Duke Roberto I of Parma through both his wives: Maria's paternal grandmother, Infanta Alicia, is the daughter of Prince Elias, one of the sons of Duke Roberto I and his first wife, Maria Pia of Bourbon-Two Sicilies; Simeon's grandmother, Empress Zita, was one of the children Duke Roberto I had with his second wife, Infanta Maria Antonia of Bragança.

Princess Inés married in Toledo in October 2001 an Italian aristocrat by the name of Nobile Michele Carelli Palombi of the Marquesses di Raiano. Two years later it was the turn of Princess Victoria, the family's youngest child, to settle down. Her choice fell on Mr. Markos Nomikos, scion of an important Greek shipbuilding family. The couple's wedding was celebrated at the Convent of the Asunción de Calatrava, in Almagro, Ciudad Real. Coincidentally, when Victoria's grandparents attended the wedding of the Prince of Asturias in Athens in 1962, the Greek court appointed Mr. P. Nomikos as their personal attaché!

From the left: the Duchess of Calabria, Princess Victoria, the Duke of Calabria, Princess Maria, Princess Cristina and Princess Inés.

Then, there is the Duke of Noto, Prince Pedro of Bourbon-Two Sicilies. As was the case with his four sisters, Pedro attended schools in Madrid. He also did his military service in the Regiment de los Monteros de Espinosa, the royal guard. Later, Pedro studied at university and for years has worked as an engineer, all while assisting his father with the successful management of La Toledana and the administration of the Constantinian Order of St. George.

At some point in 1991, the Duke of Noto met doña Sofía Landaluce y Melgarejo, a great-granddaughter of the Duke of San Fernando de Quiroga. On a side note, the title was created by King Fernando VII of Spain, son-in-law of King Francesco I of the Two Sicilies, for don Joaquín de Melgarejo y Saurín, a nobleman who married María Luisa de Borbón y Vallabriga, youngest child of Infante don Luis of Spain, former Archbishop of Toledo and Primate of Spain, and his morganatic wife María Teresa de Vallabriga. The Infante don Luis, the youngest son of King Felipe V, was also a brother King Carlos III/IV of Naples, father of King Ferdinando I. Since the 1st Duke of San Fernando de Quiroga and his Borbón wife were childless, at his death the title passed to a nephew and has since remained in the Melgarejo family.

Even though Sofía came from a distinguished family with properties near la Toledana, the Duke of Calabria had hoped

The Duke of Noto.

103

Infanta Alicia and her great-grandson Jaime, Duke of Capua.

that his son would follow tradition and settled with someone of similar rank. It was not to be for Pedro was in love with Sofía and they were set on building a life together. To avoid any sort of scandal, they settled at la Toledana, where Pedro was fully involved in running the estate. The couple's love was crowned with the birth of a son in 1993, Jaime, who was registered with the last names *"Borbón y Landaluce."* In spite of their decision to remain a couple not pleasing everyone, Pedro and Sofía were tenacious and relentless. In due course, the Infante and his wife began seeing their grandson and it is said that their love for the child, who was quite cherubic, did more than anything else to bring the Infante don Carlos to accepting his son's choice. Times were also changing across the continent and most royal and former ruling families abandoned old marriage equality requirements. Hence, in March 2001 the Duke of Noto and Sofía Landaluce contracted matrimony in a mass celebrated inside the chapel of the prestigious Real Club de Puerta de Hierro in Madrid. The wedding mass was officiated by a priest who was the grandson of the late Infanta María Cristina, youngest daughter of Uncle King. The Prince of Asturias, as well as his sister the Duchess of Lugo, with her husband, and his aunt the Infanta Margarita, Duchess of Soria, with her husband and children, was present. It was an elegant and discrete affair and neither groom nor bride, in keeping with their tendency to remain private made much fuss of it.

Two years later, the Duchess of Noto gave birth to a second son, Juan. Then in 2004 followed another son, Pablo, and three years later a fourth son, Pedro, joined the nursery. In 2008 the Duchess of Noto gave birth to their fifth child, and first daughter, Sofía. Two more daughters followed: Blanca in 2011 and Marie in 2015.

Last year, it was the Duke of Noto, supported by his mother, who sat with his cousin the Duke of Castro and signed an agreement to bring the long rift within the dynasty to an end. The signing of the reconciliation took place while many of the remaining Bourbons of the Two Sicilies traveled to Naples to attend the beatification of Queen Maria Cristina, mother of King Francesco II. The move toward reconciliation began the previous year when the Dukes of Noto and Castro, accompanied by their wives, met several times. An intermediary was also brought in and he met with the Castros several times in London and their home in Monaco. In the end, the agreement signed did not address or discuss headship of house, but both sides recognized each other's titles. *"The two branches are more concerned with the unification of the Constantinian Order,"* wrote Marlene Eilers Koenig in her report for *EUROHISTORY: The European Royal History Magazine.*

We feel it is a significant importance to publish the agreement in these pages:

The Dukes of Noto and their son the Duke of Capua.

The wedding of Princess Cristina and don Pedro López-Quesada at La Toledana. With them are the Duke of Calabria, as well as the Prince of Asturias and his sisters Infanta Elena and Infanta Cristina.

Princess Maria on her wedding day to Archduke Simeon of Austria.

Princess Inés, Nobile Michele Carelli Palombi & King Juan Carlos I.

Princess Victoria and her husband Mr. Markos Nomikos.

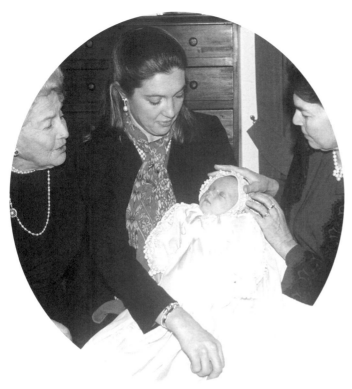

Four generations at the christening of Archduke Johannes of Austria. From left: the Countess of Paris, Archduchess Maria holding her son Johannes, the Duchess of Calabria.

Infanta Alicia and her daughter Princess Teresa, then Marquesa de Laula, now Marquesa de Laserna.

Princess Inés and her son don Manuel Morales y de Borbón.

Infanta Alicia and her grandson don Rodrigo Moreno y de Borbón.

The Duchess of Calabria and the Infanta Elena of Spain.

Princess Victoria of Bourbon-Two Sicilies,
Mrs. Markos Nomikos.

The Duchess of Calabria, Mr. López-Quesada and Princess Cristina.

The Duke and Duchess of Noto.

The Duke of Noto and the Duke of Castro after signing the "Act of Family Reconciliation," Naples, January 2014.

ACT OF FAMILY RECONCILIATION OF THE HOUSE AND DYNASTY OF BOURBON-TWO SICILIES

ON THE ONE PART HRH Prince Don Carlo of Bourbon Two Sicilies, Duke of Castro, and his Consort HRH Princess Donna Camilla, Duchess of Castro, both on their own behalf and in personal and dynastic representation, and on behalf of their daughters HRH Princess Donna Maria Carolina of Bourbon-Two Sicilies, Duchess of Palermo and HRH Princess Donna Maria Chiara of Bourbon-Two Sicilies, Duchess of Capri.

AND ON THE OTHER PART HRH Prince Don Pedro of Bourbon-Two Sicilies, Duke of Noto, on his own behalf and on behalf of His Father HRH Prince Don Carlos of Bourbon-Two Sicilies, Duke of Calabria, Infante of Spain, by whom he has been expressly delegated to complete this RECONCILIATION, together with his spouse HRH Princess Dona Sofia, Duchess of Noto, and their son HRH Prince Don Jaime of Bourbon-Two Sicilies, Duke of Capua.

BOTH PARTIES, animated by a desire for family and dynastic rapprochement and reconciliation between the two branches of the Royal House of Bourbon-Two Sicilies, which, due to historical circumstances, misunderstandings and misconceptions by family members, has been for many years the subject of disputes both personal and among its supporters:

BEING AWARE that the divisions and disputes between the two branches produced nothing except greater division and loss of prestige for the dynasty, aside from the good example of family harmony that is expected from such a distinguished Royal House.

UNDERSTANDING that on the one hand in accord with the times and because the judgment of history requires them to leave evidence of a good example and harmony and on the other hand because the division between the Constantinian knights and dames militating within the Sacred Military Constantinian Order of Saint George is harmful to the Order and its aims.

BOTH SIDES BEING AWARE of the continuous efforts of our recent Popes and, in particular, of our present Holy Father, Pope Francis, in favor of the re-evangelization of Europe and of the unity of all Christians

DECLARING their common desire for reconciliation, as a family and as Constantinians of both branches and to put an end to the rivalries and misunderstandings between family members and their supporters, in a renewed Constantinian and Catholic spirit of service to the Holy Church and spreading our Holy Faith.

CONFIDENT on the part of both that Divine Providence is charged with indicating the way to dynastic unity of the Royal House of Bourbon-Two Sicilies

AGREEING that both parties shall in the meanwhile put all their efforts to a dynastic and family commitment towards achieving a spirit of harmony and understanding not only between They but also between their followers and supporters, RECOGNIZING RESPECTIVELY AS COUSINS THE TREATMENT AND TITLES PRESENTLY USED BY BOTH PARTIES AND THEIR DESCENDANTS, ACTING PUBLICLY TOGETHER AS A SINGLE FAMILY.

And in good faith and family concord to invite to join in this ACT OF RECONCILIATION all the members of the dynasty of Bourbon-Two Sicilies, to whom both parties will make known this private ACT OF RECONCILAITION.

Signed at Naples the 24 January 2014.

Today, the Duke of Noto helms the many enterprises owned by the family. He is also very active in the administration of the Constantinian Order of St. George, while acting in his father's stead since the Infante don Carlos is affected by a debilitating illness. Pedro and Sofía's eldest son, Jaime, Duke of Capua, is gradually casting his place next to his father. He will be, we hope, the Head of a united House of the Two Sicilies.

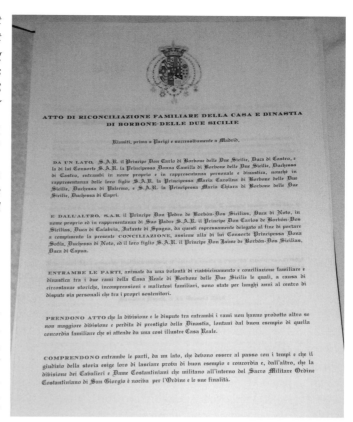

The Act of Family Reconciliation.

The Sicilian Royal Family. From left: Princess Elena, Princess Maria Cristina, Father Alessandro, Princess Anne, Prince Casimiro, Prince Luigi Alfonso, the Duke of Capua, the Duchess of Castro, the Duchess of Palermo, the Duke of Noto, the Duchess of Calabria, the Duchess of Capri, the Duke of Castro, Mrs. Crociani, Princess Teresa, the Duchess of Noto and Clara Moreno y de Borbón – Naples, January 2014.

CHAPTER *VIII*

Maria Immacolata
Princess Johann Georg of Saxony

The eldest daughter in the family and nicknamed "Gietta", Maria Immacolata, was born in 1874, and grew into an extremely personable young lady, well educated, of distinguished appearance and charming. There appeared to be no great pressure on her or indeed on any of her sisters to marry and the three who did so were older than most other Royal brides of the time. Not until her 30th birthday on October 30th 1904 did Maria Immacolata enter into matrimony with the widower Prince Johann Georg of Saxony, five years her senior and the second son of the then Crown Prince Georg of Saxony by his Portuguese wife Infanta Maria Ana, a daughter of Queen Maria II.

After being educated privately, Prince Johann Georg had studied law at the University of Freiburg-im-Breisgau, in the Black Forest region of western Germany, before switching to the University of Leipzig, where he specialized in History and the History of Art. The obligatory military career then followed, during which he attained the rank of Infantry General. In addition the Prince was an inveterate traveller and a collector of art. He was particularly interested in Egypt and the Near East and visited the region many times, returning home with many valuable artifacts and countless photographs and publishing scholarly pamphlets and booklets on his many journeys.

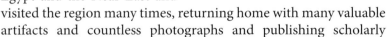

Princess Maria Immacolata.

In 1894 Johann Georg married Duchess Maria Isabella of Württemberg, daughter of Duke Philipp from the Catholic line of the family by his Habsburg wife Archduchess Maria Theresa. Isabella died 10 years later leaving a childless widower.

Johann Georg and Maria Immacolata settled in Saxony at Schloss Weesenstein, about 30 kilometers from Dresden and their tall stately figures graced many public and Royal events in the Kingdom of Saxony. They also frequently represented the Saxon Royal Family at Royal events abroad. After the ignominious departure of the troublesome and infamous Louisa of Tuscany from the Saxon Royal Court and her subsequent divorce from the future King Friedrich August

Prince Johann Georg of Saxony.

Opposite page: Princess Johann Georg of Saxony.

Princess Maria Immacolata.

Prince Johann Georg and his wife Princess Maria Immacolata.

Princess Maria Immacolata functioned as surrogate mother to the children of her brother-in-law King Friedrich August III of Saxony, whose had abandoned him. From left: Princess Anna Monika, Princess Margarete, Princess Maria Immacolata and Princess Maria Alix.

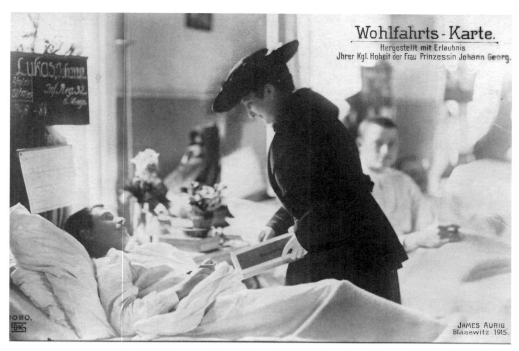

Wohlfahrts-Karte.
Hergestellt mit Erlaubnis
Jhrer Kgl. Hoheit der Frau Prinzessin Johann Georg.

JAMES AURIG
Blasewitz 1915.

Princess Maria Immacolata visiting casualties during the Great War.

III, the position of "First Lady" was vacant, and Maria Immacolata was an eminently suitable candidate for this role. Childless herself, she took to her heart the King's six motherless children and grew extremely close to them. The Princess and her husband continued to support King Friedrich August III through the difficult years of World War I, but finally in November 1918 the Saxony Monarchy, along with all its other German counterparts, fell.

Reduced to the rank of essentially private citizens, Johann Georg and Maria Immacolata decided to leave Saxony and moved to Freiburg-im-Breisgau where the Prince had studied. They acquired a sizeable villa there, large enough to accommodate the Prince's ever-growing art collections. Not without means themselves they provided valuable financial support to various of Maria Immacolata's siblings, whose monetary status was always fairly precarious. The Princess brought her aged and ailing mother the Countess of Caserta to live with her, and it was at Freiburg that Maria Antonietta died peacefully aged eighty-seven in September 1938. Two months later Johann Georg died as well whilst on a visit to the Württembergs at Altshausen. His widow survived World War II and died at Muri in Switzerland in 1947. The Prince's collection was purchased by the government of the German Land of Rheinland-Pfalz and is to be found at the Landesmuseum in Mainz.

The Royal Family of Saxony. Standing in back, from the left: Prince Johann Georg and his wife Princess Maria Immacolata, and Father Max. Seated, in the same order: Princess Mathilde, King Friedrich August III and Archduchess Maria Josepha, the widow of Archduke Otto and mother of Emperor Karl, Austria-Hungary's last monarch. Maria Josepha's husband was a first cousin of Princess Maria Immacolata.

CHAPTER *IX*

Maria Christina
Archduchess Peter Ferdinand of Austria-Tuscany

Born in 1877, Princess Maria Christina ("Titina") was the first of the Caserta daughters to marry. In November 1900 in Cannes, in a ceremony attended by members of many other Royal Houses she was married to Archduke Peter Ferdinand of Austria, third son of another dispossessed former Italian ruler, Grand Duke Ferdinand IV of Tuscany, by his second wife the former Princess Alicia of Bourbon-Parma. Peter Ferdinand's mother was one of the sisters of Duke Roberto I of Parma, father of Empress Zita of Austria, Queen of Hungary. The reader will recall that Duke Roberto I's first wife was Princess Maria Pia of Bourbon-Two Sicilies, an aunt of Maria Christina. For several generation in fact, Parmas, Tuscans, Austrians and Sicilians engaged in a high degree of endogamy, the sort that provide genealogists of royal families with untold material.

Peter Ferdinand had been brought up with a large number of siblings at the family's Austrian home in exile, the Residenz in Salzburg, and was a serving officer in the Austro-Hungarian Army. The Archduke's military career blossomed.

Archduke Peter Ferdinand and his wife spent the first years of their married life at Linz in Upper Austria, where the Archduke was garrisoned, but their main residence was in Salzburg, where Peter Ferdinand had a large villa in the suburb of Parsch. Four children were produced by this extremely happy marriage – Gottfried in 1902,

Archduchess Maria Christina.

Helene in 1903, Georg in 1905 and Rosa in 1908. The family also maintained excellent relations with Emperor Franz Joseph and the other members of the Imperial Family, and the ties were further cemented following the marriage of the future Emperor Karl to Princess Zita of Bourbon-Parma in 1911.

Furthermore, during the Great War Archduke Peter Ferdinand saw active service as Lietenant-Fieldmarshal. In June 1915, he asked to be relieved of command and again in 1916. This was due mainly to criticism lobbied against him by General Auffenberg, who accused him in his memoirs of having prevented the encirclement of the Fifth Russian Army at Komarov by awkward maneuvering. Emperor Karl, however, had full confidence in Archduke Peter Ferdinand and in 1917 appointed him General of Infantry. In his new position, Peter Ferdinand was stationed in the Tyrolean Western Front. Due to the close links of kinship Peter Ferdinand and Maria Christina shared with Emperor Karl and Empress Zita, both couples remained very close friends.

Opposite page: Archduchess Maria Christina of Austria-Tuscany.

The wedding of Princess Maria Chrisrtina of Bourbon-Two Sicilies and Archduke Peter Ferdinand of Austria-Tuscany, Cannes, 1900. Seated, fron row, from the left: Grand Duchess Anastasia Mikahilovna of Mecklenburg-Schroerin, the Duchess of Calabria (holding her daughter Maria Christina), the Countess of Caserta (with Princess Maria Anotnietta on her lap), Grand Duchess Alicia of Tuscany, the Count of Caserta, Prince Gabriele of Bourbon-Two Sicilies, Countess Maria Carolina Zamoyski, Prince Francesco di Poala of Bourbon-Two Sicilies, the Countess of Trapani, Grand Duke Ferdinando IV of Tuscany, Pricne Filippo of Bourbon-Two Sicilies and Princess Maria Giuseppina of Bourbon-Two Sicilies. Second row, standing, same order: Archduke Josef Ferdinand of Austria-Tuscany, Prince Carlo(s) of Bourbon-Two Sicilies, Archduke Leopold Ferdinand of Austria-Tuscany, the Count of Bardi, Archduke Heinrich Ferdinand of Austria-Tuscany, Prince Friedrich August of Saxony, the Duke of Calabria, Duke Roberto 1 of Parma, Princess Louisa of Saxony, Princess Maria Pia of Bourbon-Two Sicilies and slightly behind is her sister Princess Maria Immacolata, Archduchess Germana of Austria-Tuscany and slightly behind her is her sister Archduchess Margarete, the nealyweds, Archduchess Anna of Austria-Tuscany, unidentified, unidentified, Count Andrzej Zamoyski, unidentified, unidentified, Prince Ranieri of Bourbon-Two Sicilies. Third row, same order: unidentified, Fürstin Marie Louise zu Isenburg, unidentified,

After the fall of the Austro-Hungarian Monarchy in late 1918, Peter Ferdinand, extremely loyal to the Emperor, refused to sign the necessary documents recognising the Republic and renouncing his rights, and chose to go into exile. His villa in Salzburg and other possessions were confiscated by the new republican authorities. He received no compensation and the villa was subsequently demolished. Peter Ferdinand and his family moved to Switzerland, where they lived for almost twenty years in straightened financial circumstances. In 1935, the Austrian Government under Chancellor Schuschnigg repealed the Habsburg exile laws, and the family quietly returned to Austria, settling in a country house on the banks of Lake Wolfgang near St. Gilgen. Due to his service during the Great War, the Schuschnigg government granted the Archduke a small pension that contributd to imnmproving the family's reduced circumstances. After the Nazi "Anschluss" of Austria the Habsburg Laws were reimposed but the Archduke was left in peace by the

Archduke Peter Ferdinand of Austria-Tuscany.

authorities. On the death of his elder brother Joseph Ferdinand in 1942 he became the Head of the Tuscany Line of the House of Habsburg and "de jure" Grand Duke of Tuscany. Archduchess Maria Christina died in 1947, her husband a year later and both are buried in the town cemetery in St. Gilgen.

Their elder son Gottfried married Princess Dorothea of Bavaria in 1938. She was one of the daughters of Prince Franz and and Princess Isabella, a Croÿ by birth. One of her sisters, Marie, was married to Prince Pedro Henrique d'Orléans-Bragança, whose mother was Princess Maria Pia of Bourbon-Two Sicilies, Archduchess Maria Christina's younger sister. Worth mentioning as well is the fact that Gottfried's children, through maternal line, are first cousins of Princess Gisela of Bavaria, the wife of Alexander, Margrave of Meißen, Head of House Saxony

Archduchess Maria Christina.

Archduke Peter Ferdinand.

Peter Ferdinand and Maria Christina's younger son Archduke Georg married in 1936 Countess Marie-Valerie von Waldburg-Zeil, a great-granddaughter of Emperor Franz Joseph.

Both of Peter Ferdinand and Maria Christina's daughters were destined to marry the same groom, Duke Philipp-Albrecht of Württemberg, whose mother was Archduchess Margarete Sophie of Austria, only daughter of Princess Maria Annunziata of Bourbon-Two Sicilies, a sister of the Count of Caserta. The elder daughter Archduchess Helene married Duke Philipp-Albrecht in 1923 but died in childbirth the following year. Her child, Duchess Marie Christine, survived and married Prince Georg of Liechtenstein, by whom she had several children. The younger daughter, Archduchess Rosa married her widower

The family of Archduke Peter Ferdinand of Austria-Tuscany. Clockwise from top: Archduke Peter Ferdinand, Archduchess Helene, Archduke Georg, Archduchess Maria Christina, Archduchess Rosa and Archduke Gottfried.

brother-in-law in 1928. The couple had six children, most of them having made notable marriages into other royal families. For example, Princess Elisabeth, Rosa and Philipp-Albrecht's second daughter, married back into the Sicilian Royal Family when she wed Prince Antonio of Bourbon-Two Sicilies, eldest son of Prince Gabriele

Peter Ferdinand with his children: Gottfried, Georg and Helene.

Archduke Peter Ferdinand during the Great War.

Archduchess Maria Christina.

Archduke Gottfried.

and his first wife Princess Malgorzata Czartoryska. Two others, Marie Thérèse and Carl, also married Bourbons, but from the Orléans branch of the family: Marie Thérèse was married to Prince Henri, Count de Clermont (the present Count of Paris), while Carl, the present Head of House Württemberg, is married to Princess Diane, sister of both the present Count of Paris and the Duchess of Calabria, the former Princess Anne d'Orléans.

Peter Ferdinand and Maria Christina's many descendants live throughout Europe, and their great-grandson Archduke Sigismund is the present Head of the Grand Ducal House of Tuscany, while two other great-grandsons, Friedrich and Jean, will be the Heads of the Royal Houses of Württemberg and France, respectively.

Top left: Duke Philipp Albrecht on his wedding day to Archduchess Rosa of Austria-Tuscany. With them is his daughter Marie Christine.

Top right: Duchess Marie Chritine of Württemberg and Prince George of Liechtenstein.

Left: Archduke Gottfried, eldest son of Archduke Peter Ferdinand and Archduchess Maria Christina with his wife Princess Dorothea of Bavaria.

Bottom left: Archduchess Helen of Austria-Tuscany, who was the first wife of Duke Philipp Albrecht of Württemberg, whose second wife was her sister Rosa.

Below: Archduke Georg of Austria-Tuscany.

CHAPTER X

Maria Pia
Princess Luiz d'Orléans-Bragança

Princess Maria Pia.

Princess Maria Pia, born in 1878, small in stature and dark in complexion, was the most "Mediterranean" of the Caserta daughters. She also married comparatively late in life, at the age of 30. Her long wait to marry the man of her choice, Prince Luiz d'Orléans-Bragança was due to dynastic complications in the Imperial Family of Brazil.

The Brazilian Empire had fallen in 1889 and the Imperial Family banished. Days after his overthrow, Emperor Pedro II, his family and their closest supporters sailed away to Europe, where Empress Teresa Christina died soon after arriving in Portugal. Emperor Pedro II died in 1891, his heir being his elder daughter the Princess Imperial Isabel. She had married a member of the French Royal Family, Prince Gaston d'Orléans, Count d'Eu, and the couple had three sons: Pedro de Alcântara born in 1875, Luiz born in 1878 and Antonio born in 1881. The family lived in France. There the Count d'Eu acquired a large residence in Boulogne-sur-Seine near Paris, while initially renting from one of his Orléans cousins, and later purchasing, the estate and Château d'Eu in Normandy.

In the early 1900s the second son Luiz paid a visit to the Casertas at Cannes. He and Princess Maria Pia were immediately attracted to each other and began to plan to marry. Prince Luiz's elder brother Pedro had also fallen in love with the attractive Bohemian Countess Elisabeth Dobrzensky von Dobrzenicz. Although of excellent character and from an excellent family of the Austrian high nobility, Elisabeth was not considered to be of equal birth by the Princess Imperial, who wished a Royal Princess for her eldest son. She imposed a five years waiting time for the couple to reflect on their feelings for each other, and Prince Luiz and Princess Maria Pia imposed a similar waiting time on themselves. When the time was up, both couples were unchanged in their desire to marry. On October 30, 1908, Pedro signed a document renouncing his rights as first-born son. Then Luiz and Maria Pia married in Cannes on November 4, 1908 and Pedro and Elisabeth were married in a quieter ceremony at Versailles ten days later. This *"marital renunciation"* has caused as much dissent in the Brazilian Imperial Family as occurred with the Two Sicilies and the Act of Cannes. Other property dealings between the eldest sons of Pedro de Alcântara and Luiz, Pedro Gastão and Pedro Henrique were only to add discord to an already volatile situation.

Prince Luiz and Princess Maria Pia first made their home at Boulogne-sur-Seine, an affluent suburb

Opposite page: Princess Maria Pia d'Orléans Bragança

122

Gia di Bourbon Sicile
Orléans Braga

of Paris, where two of their three children, Pedro Henrique (1909) Luiz Gastão (1911) and Pia Maria (1913) were born. The children were raised between Paris, Eu and Cannes. They were devoted to their grandparents, in whose homes they lived for quite a considerable part of their childhood. At Eu they rode and hunted, while also spending a great part of the day outdoors. Life at Boulogne-sur-Seine was a bit more restrained for at some point life lived outside had to be traded for education and preparation for the future. In Cannes, where the Casertas led a much simpler existence, the children swam, ran, played tennis and enjoyed the Villa Marie Thérèse's large gardens. Princess Pia Maria, who wrote her memoirs many years later, fondly remembered a golden childhood only interrupted by the occasional tragedy, like the death of her Eu grandparents and that of poor Prince Luiz, her father.

An intelligent, active and personable man, Luiz took his position as heir to the Brazilian throne seriously. In 1907 he attempted to return to the country, but

The wedding of Princess Maria Pia of Bourbon-Two Sicilies and Prince Luiz d'Orléans-Bragança.

was forbidden by the Republican authorities from disembarking at Rio de Janeiro. At the outset of the First World War, he and his brother Antonio, forbidden by law from serving in the French armed forces, became officers in the British army and air force. In the trenches in Flanders, Luiz unfortunately contracted a virulent form of rheumatism, which later spread to his bones and rendered him incapable of walking. Medicine at the time could do nothing to help him and his condition led to his untimely death in 1920, at the age of only forty-two years old. On the death of the Princess Imperial in 1921, the young Prince Pedro Henrique became Head of the Imperial House of Brazil.

Opposite page: Prince Luiz d'Orléans-Bragança.

Interestingly, the following year, the Brazilian Imperial Family, led by the aged Count d'Eu, sailed

off to Brazil since the government had allowed their return after more than three decades of exile. Sadly, the Count d'Eu died during the journey and never got to see Brazil again. Some family members returned to France with his remains and the Parisian period of Maria Pia's family came to an end as she settled permanently on the French Riviera after her father-in-law's death.

In Cannes, Princess Maria Pia brought up her children single-handedly, aided by the considerable fortune left behind by her in-laws, which was shared with her brother-in-law Pedro de Alcântara. After the sale of the Villa Marie Thérèse, when her parents moved to a smaller home, Maria Pia had a house constructed for herself and her children. Named "Mas St Louis" and located in Mandelieu,

Prince Luiz d'Orléans-Bragança and his sons Pedro Henrique and Luiz Gastão at the beach in Cannes, where the family spent long periods with the Counts of Caserta.

As was the case with other royalty all around Europe at the time, Prince Luiz d'Orléans-Bragança became an enthusiastic motorist. In this image we see him in his car with his wife Maria Pia. Seated behind them, perhaps a bit apprehensively, are the Count and Countess of Caserta.

The Brazilian Imperial Family. Standing from left: the Prince of Grão Pará, Prince Antonio and Princess Maria Pia. At front, same order: Princess Teresa, Princess Elisabeth holding Prince João, Princess Isabelle, Prince Pedro de Alcantâra, the Count d'Eu, the Princess Imperial of Brazil, Princess Pia Maria, Prince Luiz, Prince Luiz Gastão and Prince Pedro Henrique.

she settled there for the rest of her life.

Tragedy, never far from the Bourbons of the Two Sicilies, now paid Princess Maria Pia a most unwelcome visit. Her middle child Prince Luiz Gastão contacted an illness the zapped him of all energy and caused him great physical deterioration. His sister described Luiz Gastão as the more attractive of the two brothers for he was, *"beautiful, tall, he had the looks and the blue eyes famous among the Orléans. He possessed a character that showed rectitude without fail."* The young man was taken to Paris were the capital's best doctors tried to help him, but little could be done to save his life. Luiz Gastão died on September 8,1931. Maria Pia and her remaining children were devastated by this second, severe loss within their small family circle. Luiz Gastão was irreplaceable and his absence was

The Count d'Eu and the Princess Imperial with Prince Luiz and Princess Maria Pia behind them. The children, from left: Pedro Henrique, Pia Maria and Luiz Gastão.

127

The wedding of Prince Pedro Henrique d'Orléans-Bragança and Princess Maria of Bavaria, Schloß Nymphenburg, August 19, 1937. From left, down the staircase: Prince Engelbert of Croÿ (partly cut off). Prince Anton of Croÿ, Luitpold Duke on Bavaria, Prince Karl of Croÿ, Prince Josef Clemens of Bavaria, Prince Albrecht of Bavaria, Senhor de Sampaio, Mr. Doyen, Countess Carolina de Silva Ramos. Next to the lion's statue: Princess Maria Giuseppina of Bourbon-Two Sicilies, Princess Klara of Bavaria, the Duchess de Talavera de la Reina, Count Jas Zamoyski. Standing, from left: Princess Editha of Bavaria, Princess Maria Antonietta of Bourbon-Two Sicilies, Princess Irmingard of Bavaria, Princess Bona of Bavaria, Princess Adelgunde of Bavaria, Princess Urraca of Bourbon-Two Sicilies, the Countess di Villa Colli, Princess Cecilia of Bourbon-Two Sicilies, Princess Dorothea of Bavaria, Princess Marie Elisabeth of Croÿ, Infante Fernando Maria of Spain, Countess Theresa von Preysing, the groom, Archduke Georg of Austria-Tuscany, Princess Eleonore of Bavaria, the Prince of Asturias (obstructed), Prince Anton of Croÿ, Prince Ludwig of Bavaria, Prince Gabriele of Bourbon-Two Sicilies, Princess Pia Maria d'Orléans-Bragança, Princess Lucia of Bourbon-Two Sicilies, Duke Philipp Albrecht of Württemberg (obstructed), Princess Engelbert of Croÿ, Princess Albrecht of Bavaria, Princess Ludwig Ferdinand of Bavaria, Infante Luis of Spain, Princess Cristina of Bourbon-Two Sicilies, unidentified, Princess Helmtrud of Bavaria, Infanta Mercedes of Spain, Prince Johann Georg of Saxony, Princess Maria Immacolata of Bourbon-Two Sicilies, Princess Esperanza of Bourbon-Two Sicilies, Prince Konrad of Bavaria, Infanta Isabel Alfonsa of Spain, Prince Gennaro of Bourbon-Two Sicilies, Prince Adalbert of Bavaria, the Duchess of Urach. Seated, same order: Princess Hildegard of Bavaria, Infanta Luisa of Spain, Fürstin Adelgunde of Hohenzollern, Princess Alfons of Bavaria, the Countess of Paris, Prince Franz and Princess Isabella

From left: Princess Maria Pia d'Orléans-Bragança, Prince Franz of Bavaria, Princess Pia Maria d'Orléans-Bragança (obstructed), the Count of Paris, the newlyweds, King Alfonso XIII of Spain, Crown Princess Antonia of Bavaria, Princess Isabella of Bavaria, Crown Prince Rupprecht of Bavaria, the Duke of Calabria and the Countess of Paris.

felt forever. Maria Pia, deeply devout and pious, found solace and comfort in yearly pilgrimages to Lourdes.

As the decade of the 1930s progressed, it was time for the children to build families of their own. Prince Pedro Henrique had been educated in France, where he also attended the prestigious Ecôle des Sciences Politiques in Paris. His Brazilian grandmother described him as, *"a very intelligent child,"* and one who would certainly be able to successfully carry the historical legacy he inherited. Prince Pedro Henrique was the first one to find a bride and settle down. In doing so he did not go far and in August 1937 he married Princess Maria of Bavaria. She was one of the daughters of Prince Franz of Bavaria and his wife, the former Princess Isabella of Croÿ. Born at Schloß Nymphenburg in September 1914, Maria was raised in Bavaria. Her sister Dorothea would also enter the family of the Count and Countess of Caserta, when in 1938 she married Archduke Gottfried of Austria-Tuscany, Prince Pedro Henrique's first cousin. The couple soon enough welcomed their first child, a boy named Luiz Gastão, in honor of his Brazilian grandfather and uncle. In due time, Princess Maria had eleven more children, the eight youngest all being born in Brazil, where the family settled after the end of the Second World War.

A rather complicated financial transaction Pedro Henrique entered into with his cousin Pedro Gastão somehow caused him the loss of a considerable portion of his inheritance. It remains a complicated matter. This deal, plus Pedro Gastão's decision to challenge his cousin's rights to the inexistent Brazilian throne, caused the family rift to deepen. Hence, once settled in Brazil, Pedro Henrique eventually moved from Petropolis to a farm he purchased in Jacarezinho, Paraná State, where he became a farmer. Years later, he moved to Vassouras in the State of Rio de Janeiro, an important region for coffee production. He died there in July 1981. Princess Maria continued living in Brazil, with occasional visits to Europe, where several of her children settled. She died in 2011, nearly thirty tears after her husband's death.

Prince Luiz Gastão d'Orléans-Bragança.

During the Second World War, Princess Maria Pia remained in Mandelieu, where along with her daughter they experienced

129

From left: Prince Pedro Henrique, Prince Luiz Gastão, Princess Maria Pia and Princess Pia Maria d'Orléans-Bragança.

considerable privations. One of the reasons keeping her there was the fact that her unmarried sister, Maria Giuseppina, holding Italian citizenship, was not allowed leaving the area. In due course, Maria Pia left Mandelieu and joined Pedro Henrique at La Bourbole, a protected zone, where living conditions were far better, particularly for larger families. These were difficult times for the family as the war raging across Europe caused untold suffering, particularly for those caught in the destruction ravaging Eastern Europe. That April 1944, Maria Pia became a grandmother for the third time when Princess Maria gave birth to a daughter, Isabelle, named thus in honor of their cousin the Countess of Paris. Yet, as it so often seemed to happen to the Bourbons of the Two Sicilies, one great joy was followed by a loss. Six days after the arrival of Princess Isabelle, the family received news that Prince Gennaro, Maria Pia's brother, passed away in Cannes, where he lived with his morganatic wife Beatrice Bordessa, the Countess di Villa Colli.

Maria Pia returned to Mandelieu at the end of 1944 and she was back at home when the war came to an end. It was a time of mixed emotions: Italy was liberated; Vienna fell to the Russians, as did Poland and Czechoslovakia. The Allies landed in Normandy and the Germans retreated from France and into Germany for a last stand. Destruction reigned supreme and

Princess Maria Pia d'Orléans-Bragança.

countless cousins and friends lost all they owned and became penniless exiles desperate to settle down, grow roots and rebuild their dislocated lives. Pedro Henrique achieved that by relocating to Brazil, while Maria Pia and her daughter decided to do so where they were happiest, in Mandelieu.

Pia Maria married French Count Rene de Nicolay, owner of the magnificent Château de Lude, in 1948. The couple met in Locarno, where Maria Pia and her daughter had traveled to meet the Duke of Calabria, who was spending time there. Pia Maria, who by then was in her mid-thirties hesitated to accept René's marriage proposal as she feared leaving her mother alone. Her mind was changed when he told her, *"your mother will have her own rooms at Lude, near us."* Unfortunately, he died six years later, leaving her a widow with young children. She took over the administration of her husband's estate and died there in October 2000 after a very successful life.

Prince Pedro Henrique and Princess Maria d'Orléans-Bragança.

Princess Maria Pia lived to a great age and died at Mandelieu in 1973, aged ninety-four.

Prince Pedro Henrique and Princess Maria d'Orléans-Braganza with their twelve children.

CHAPTER **XI**

Maria Giuseppina

The youngest daughter, born in 1880, was universally known by her nickname "Beppa." She was destined not to marry and stayed at home to look after her parents, although she did serve as a Red Cross nurse during World War I, when many injured allied soldiers were sent to Cannes to convalesce.

This use of having the family's youngest daughter remain unmarried seems to have been rather common at the time. Queen Victoria, for example, tried her best, unsuccessfully as it turned out, to keep her youngest daughter unmarried. Queen Alexandra was more successful in doing so and Princess Victoria remained under her mother's clutches. Another example was that of Queen Louise of Denmark, consort of King Frederik VIII, who showed little interest in finding her two youngest daughters any husbands,

Opposite page: In back, from left: Princess Maria Giuseppina, the Countess of Caserta and Princess Maria Pia d'Orléans-Bragança. Seated, same order: Princess Maria Immacolata of Saxony and Archduchess Maria Christina of Austria-Tuscany.

even still, one of the princesses in question managed to get away from her mother. Other daughters facing the same future, such as Grand Duchess Olga Alexandrovna, were luckier and escaped.

Maria Giuseppina did however maintain extremely good relations with all her siblings and visited them and their families often in Austria and Germany. She was a beloved aunt and much in favor with the family at large. Her eldest sister Maria Immacolata helped her to build a bungalow at Mandelieu, next to her siblings Gennaro and Maria Pia.

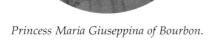

Princess Maria Giuseppina of Bourbon.

Opposite page: Princess Maria Giuseppina of Bourbon-Two Sicilies.

Marie Josepha de
Bourbon Sicilies

CHAPTER *XII*

Prince Gennaro Count di Villa Colli

The least known of the sons, Prince Gennaro, born in 1882, was the only boy in the family to opt for a Naval rather than an Army career in Spain.

In 1895, the Counts of Caserta visited Queen Regent María Cristina at Miramar Palace in San Sebastian. Along with them came young Prince Gennaro, who was studying in preparation for the entry exams for the Spanish Royal navy. His examination, successful we might add, took place in April 1898, and after that he entered the navy. By 1901 he was guard on the "Nautilus," a training vessel. Along with him was Prince Ferdinand d'Orléans, Duke de Montpensier, another royal sailor serving in Spain.

In 1904 Prince Gennaro was part of the entourage accompanying King Alfonso XIII on an official visit to the island of Mallorca, and during the remaining years of the Spanish monarch's long reign, Gennaro could be seen at court frequently, while also being present at many family gatherings. In 1910, for example, he was chosen as the godfather of his niece María de las Mercedes, who later became the mother of King Juan Carlos.

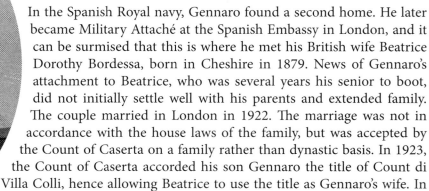

Prince Gennaro of Bourbon-Two Sicilies.

By 1909 Gennaro, already a naval officer, Gennaro boarded the frigate "Numancia" in Melilla and went to fight in the war in Morocco. Montpensier, also a naval officer, came along.

In the Spanish Royal navy, Gennaro found a second home. He later became Military Attaché at the Spanish Embassy in London, and it can be surmised that this is where he met his British wife Beatrice Dorothy Bordessa, born in Cheshire in 1879. News of Gennaro's attachment to Beatrice, who was several years his senior to boot, did not initially settle well with his parents and extended family. The couple married in London in 1922. The marriage was not in accordance with the house laws of the family, but was accepted by the Count of Caserta on a family rather than dynastic basis. In 1923, the Count of Caserta accorded his son Gennaro the title of Count di Villa Colli, hence allowing Beatrice to use the title as Gennaro's wife. In due time, Beatrice became a much appreciated member of the family, known as "Aunt Bee." Since the marriage, however, was not accorded equality, had they had any offspring,

Prince Gennaro during his childhood.

Opposite page: Prince Gennaro of Bourbon-Two Sicilies.

The coming of age of King Alfonso XIII, Palacio de Oriente, Madrid, 1902. Standing in, from left: Prince Louis of Monaco, Prince Albrecht of Prussia, the Princess of Asturias, the Duke of Calabria, Prince Eugen of Sweden, the Duchess of Calabria, Infante Carlos of Spain, the Duke of Genoa and Prince Christian of Denmark. Seated, same order: Queen Mother María Cristina of Spain, the Duke of Connaught, Infante Isabel (Countess of Girgenti), Grand Duke Vladimir Alexandrovich, Infanta Eulalia of Spain. Seated on the ground, usual order: Archduke Karl Stephan of Austria, the Crown Prince of Siam, Prince Nicholas of Greece, King Alfonso XIII of Spain, Prince Gennaro of Bourbon-Two Sicilies, the Duke de Montpensier, Infanta María Teresa of Spain.

Gennaro and Beatrice's children would not have been in the line of succession. Gennaro is worth mentioning, was not the only one of the Caserta brothers to die childless since the same happened to the family's second Francesco.

In 1873 the Countess of Caserta gave birth to her third son, a boy named Francesco. Unfortunately, the Casertas first Cannes-born child did not live long and he died in 1876. As it happened is several families, the parents later gave the same name to another son, this second Francesco being born at Cannes in 1888, a dozen years after the death of his namesake brother. Sadly, this second Francesco was destined to also have a short life. He appears to have suffered from the scourge of tuberculosis, an illness that, back then, was nearly a death sentence. The parents to a clinic in Montreux, Switzerland, where it was hoped both climate and the best medical attention available would help him recover, sent Francesco. Unfortunately, that was not the case and he died in March 1914, some weeks after turning twenty-six years old.

In 1924 Gennaro was granted Spanish nationality by King Alfonso XIII with the title "Príncipe de Borbón" and the style "Royal Highness." A few years before, Gennaro became a member of the Order of Alcántara, while in 1919 King Alfonso XIII granted him the Golden Fleece. In 1927 he rose to the rank of captain, but in 1931, after the fall of the monarchy, he left Spain permanently and settled in Cannes.

Gennaro purchased a plot of land at Mandelieu, next to his sisters Maria Pia and Maria Giuseppina. He had a villa constructed there and with Beatrice by his side it became their home. A newspaper notice from the time listed their place of residence as Mandelieu and their home was called "Villa La Casucha."

A family gathering at the Villa Marie Thérèse, Cannes. From the left: Prince Gennaro, Princess Maria Pia, Prince Francesco, Countess of Caserta, Princess Maria Giuseppina, the Duchess of Calabria with her daughters Maria Christina and Maria Antonietta, the Duke of Calabria, Prince Gabriele and the Count of Caserta.

During the German occupation both Gennaro and Beatrice did not hesitate to express their anti-Nazi opinions to anyone who cared to hear them. Even when cautioned to keep their opinions private, the couple lost little effort in expressing their utter disgust with Vichy France and with the German occupation. How they managed to remain from getting arrested and summarily dealt with, given the political climate is still a conundrum. Tragedy struck in 1944, when Gennaro was knocked down and seriously injured by a lorry from a German military convoy on the street outside the house. He lingered on, devotedly tended by his wife, but in the end succumbed to his injuries.

Some years later, the widowed Countess di Villa Colli decided that it was time to sell "La Casucha" and return to England. By then only a faint memory remained of the Bourbons of the Two Sicilies of the Villa Marie Thérèse as the family was reduced to just a few aging longtime inhabitants around Cannes, like Maria Pia and Maria Giuseppina. Beatrice died at West Malling in Kent in 1963.

CHAPTER XIII

Ranieri
Duke of Castro

Prince Ranieri, Duke of Castro.

Prince Ranieri, born in Cannes in December 1883, had an early life undistinguishable from that of his elder brothers and was also destined for a military career in Spain. After attending the Military Academy for Cavalry in Valladolid he received his commission as an officer. An excellent horseman and polo-player, he was particularly close to the young King Alfonso XIII, being only two years his senior, and his picture is often to be seen in the background at innumerable Spanish Royal Family gatherings.

Ranieri was nearly forty years old when he married his first cousin, Polish-born Countess Carolina Zamoyski, whose mother, also named Carolina, was the sister of the Countess of Caserta. Carolina was thirteen years her husband's junior. Also, the groom and the bride were first cousins, not an uncommon alliance in the House of the Two Sicilies, as the reader by now has surmised. Not surprisingly the Count of Caserta recognized this marriage as equal for Two Sicilies succession purposes. King Alfonso XIII, a stickler about these matters, did not accept the union as equal and thus the children were non-dynasts in Spain. The Zamoyskis, however, were among the most illustrious of the Polish aristocratic families and owners of vast estates. The family dates to the XV century when one Tomasz Lazinsky acquired an estate at Stary Zamosc, from where the family eventually took its name. The Zamoyskis remained prominent Polish politicians and men of government and arts. In due time, the Holy Roman Emperor elevated them to the title of counts in appreciation for their loyalty to Habsburg rule, a dynasty they had initially opposed in defense of Polish sovereignty.

After his wedding Ranieri left the Spanish Army and settled for a while on one of the Zamoyski properties at Podzamcze, where both of his children were born Maria del Carmen was born in 1924, while Ferdinando arrived nearly two years later. After the birth of their son, Prince Ranieri and Princess Carolina did not have any more children.

Life in faraway Poland did not suit Prince Ranieri. He longed for the warmth that the French Riviera and his beloved Spain provided so freely. Hankering to return to the South of France in the late 1920s, financially aided by his sister Princess Johann Georg of Saxony, Ranieri acquired a large agricultural property, Saint Sauveur, near Roquebrune-sur-Argens in the French department of Var, and not far from

Opposite page: Prince Ranieri of Bourbon-Two Sicilies.

his parents in Cannes. Here he and his family lived a quiet and hard-working existence, necessary to fund their lifestyle.

After the declaration of a Republic in Spain in 1931 and King Alfonso's departure into exile, the army pensions ceased, not only for Ranieri, but his other brothers as well. The financial situation worsened after the Second World War when any income from Carolina's estates in Poland dried up following that country's seizure by the Communists. Eventually the family had to give up Saint Sauveur and move to a smaller establishment, the Domaine de la Combe.

After the death of his brother Ferdinando, Duke of Calabria, Ranieri came forward to claim the Headship of the House of the Two Sicilies and assumed the title of Duke of Castro. His late brother, the Duke of Calabria, had accepted that this was going to be how the succession was settled as neither accepted their nephew Alfonso's decision to reject the Act of Cannes, since it had never been necessary to begin with. Alfonso's actions on the succession matter, which he had already announced to his uncles in 1949 after his father's death, did not sit well with them. Calabria's death had simply brought to the fore what was expected: the family rift widened deeply and everyone, whether they liked to or not, was forced to take sides.

The wedding of Prince Ranieri of Bourbon-Two Sicilies and his first cousin Polish-born Countess Carolina Zamoyski. The Duke of Castro was vehement in his position and never accepted his nephew Infante Alfonso's decision regarding the Act of Cannes. Many other Heads of House sided with him, perhaps most vociferously among them the Count of Paris, who did not hesitate to let his position known. The Count of Paris was not alone in this position, *"as many other Heads of House, as well as ruling monarchs and even the Italian government"* recognized Ranieri's position. One very respectable author has also mentioned that even the Papacy recognized Ranieri's claims. Hence, the rift between the Carlos and Ranieri branches deepened and would remain unbridged until well after many of its protagonists had departed from the scene.

The Duke and Duchess of Castro had two children, Maria del Carmen and Ferdinando, both born at Podzamcze, Poland, one of several Zamoyski estates scattered across that country. Eventually, the Duke of Castro decided to relocate to the French Riviera, where the couple acquired an agricultural estate. They were in France when Poland fell to the advancing and devastating onslaught of the Red Army.

Furthermore, *"Faced with a potentially distasteful dispute initiated by their cousin, and suspecting that he would exploit the situation, the other Bourbon-Two Sicilies princes and princesses made declarations in favor of the line of Prince Ranieri. This is not a secret; the declarations have been published."* No one has ever suggested that the declarations, in themselves, *"constitute dynastic law, only that they reflect reality and indicate the recognition by the other members of the royal family that Prince Ranieri, not Infante Alfonso, was head of the dynasty and grand master of the Constantinian Order of St. George."* The signatories were Prince Gabriele, Prince Antonio, Prince Casimiro, the late Prince Giovanni and the late Prince Ferdinando, all of the Two Sicilies dynasts living in 1962. Made on June 6, 1962, the declaration was also signed by the late Princess Urraca, who had also signed, with several other princesses of the Two Sicilies (sisters and daughters of Ferdinando Pio), an earlier declaration in 1960. *"Clearly, they considered it important to make their position known and, as already stated, it reflected a situation already known in their family,"* wrote one of the more spirited

Top left and right: The Duke of Castro with his only grandson, Prince Carlo of Bourbon-Two Sicilies.

Left: The Duke of Castro in old age.

Below: The Duchess of Castro and King Umberto II of Italy.

Opposite page: Prince Ranieri of Bourbon-Two Sicilies, Duke of Castro.

The wedding of Prince Ferdinand of Bourbon-Two Sicilies and Mlle. Chantal de Chevron-Villette, Giez, Haute Savoie, July 23, 1949.

supporters of the Ranieri line. Luckily, for all involved, both dynasts and their supporters, these issues are no longer fueling the family's discord.

The long marriage of Prince Ranieri and Princess Carolina came to an end in May 1968. She had been previously diagnosed with cancer and the medical team taking care of the princess could do little to stop the ravages of her illness. Princess Carolina, Duchess of Castro, died in Marseille, just a few months before the couple's forty-fifth wedding anniversary. Prince Ranieri, Duke of Castro, survived his wife by nearly five years, dying at the Domaine de la Combe in January 1973. Just six weeks before, the august prince had celebrated his eighty-ninth birthday. The couple is buried in the family tomb in the cemetery of Grand Jas in Cannes.

Princess Maria del Carmen, known as "Carmen," remained unmarried and remains alive. In July 2014 she celebrated her ninetieth birthday. Carmen of Bourbon-Two Sicilies is one of the last remnants from a bygone era of the Royal Family of the Two Sicilies.

Upon Prince Ranieri's death his only son Ferdinando inherited the claim to the Headship of the House and also assumed the Castro title.

Ferdinando had married a member of the French aristocracy, Chantal de Chevron-Villette, in 1949. Initially, the Head of House Two Sicilies, the Duke of Calabria, did not recognize the alliance as equal. This position he changed a year later when not only did he retroactively recognized the marriage as equal but also accorded Chantal the title of princess with the style of "Royal Highness."

While not descended from royal lineage, Chantal de Chevron-Villette came from an old aristocratic family that had owned estates in Provence. Her family, *of chivalric origins, originated in Bougey, Savoy.* They received the title of Barons in 1706.

Prince Ferdinando with his bride and her father, Count Pierre de Chevron-Villette.

Anyhow, Ferdinando was also an agriculturalist in the South of France, but also made regular visits to the former Two Sicilies territories in Italy, being particularly well-received in Naples. For many years, Ferdinando, as Duke of Castro, served as Grand Master of the Constantinian Order of St. George, the same position in which his cousin Infante Carlos, Duke of Calabria, served. The rift caused by Infante Alfonso's decision to disregard the Act of Cannes as a valid document, led to the Constantinian Order being divided in two: one side headed by the Duke of Castro, while the other was under the control of the Duke of Calabria. This issue is now, finally, being solved with the present Dukes of Castro and Noto agreeing to work toward becoming co-Grand Masters of the Constantinian

Standing: the Duke of Castro, Princess Carmen and Ferdinando. Seated: the Duchess of Castro, Princess Beatrice, and Princess Chantal holding Princess Anne.

Princess Carmen of Bourbon-Two Sicilies.

Princess Beatrice of Bourbon-Two Sicilies.

Order, thus bringing about an end to the rift that divided the Sicilian Royal Family for so many decades.

The Duchess of Castro, who was not only very approachable, but also very willing to correspond with royalty watchers, sadly passed away in 2005. She had turned eighty years old just a few months before. The Duke of Castro survived his wife by only three years, passing away in March 2008.

Ferdinando and Chantal had three children: Beatrice, Anne and Carlo.

Princess Beatrice was born at Saint-Raphäel, Var, in June 1950. After attending school, she settled in Paris, where she has remained most of her life working in various positions and gaining widespread respect. In fact, it is common to see Princess Beatrice appearing on the pages of the French capital's most renowned magazines. In 1978 Princess Beatrice married Prince Charles Napoléon, eldest son of Louis, Prince Napoléon, and of his wife, Princess Alix, née de Foresta. Louis was the Head of the Imperial House of Napoléon

Princess Beatrice of Bourbon-Two Sicilies and her children, Prince Jean-Christophe Napoléon and Princess Caroline.

Princess Anne and Baron Jacques Cochin on their wedding day. Behind them are the Countess of Barcelona and King Umberto II of Italy.

Princess Anne of Bourbon-Two Sicilies and her children, Nicolas and Dorothée Cochin.

for over seven decades, starting from his father's death in 1926 and ending with his own in 1997. Louis, who very successfully managed his considerable inheritance and wide investments, was the only son of Victor, Prince Napoléon, and Princess Clementine of Belgium, youngest daughter of King Leopold II and his wife the former Archduchess Marie Henriette of Austria. Hence, as a descendant of King Louis Philippe and Queen Marie Amélie, Charles also descended from King Ferdinando I and Queen Maria Carolina, founders of the Sicilian Royal Family. Nearly two years after their wedding, Charles and Beatrice became the parents of a daughter, Caroline, born near Paris in October 1980. The couple had a second child, Jean Christophe, six years later. Princess Beatrice and Prince Charles divorced in 1989. They became grandparents in 2010 when their daughter Caroline gave birth to her first child, Elvire. Caroline, easily one of the most beautiful princesses of her generation, had married the previous year Eric Quérénet-Onfroy de Bréville. A second child, Augustin, was born in 2013. Prince Jean Christophe, who was chosen by his grandfather to succeed him as Head of House Napoléon, is unmarried. He works in banking and currently lives in New York City, although he is frequently seen in Europe.

Princess Anne of Bourbon-Two Sicilies.

The Duke of Castro surrounded by members of his family. Standing, from left: Prince Antonio, Nicolas Cochin, Princess Anne, the Duke of Calabria, the Duke of Castro, Princess Caroline Napoléon, Princess Beatrice and Prince Giovanni. Seated, from left: the Duchess of Castro and Princess Urraca. Seated on the floor: Dorothée Cochin and Prince Jean-Christophe Napoléon.

Princess Anne was born at Saint-Raphäel in 1957. Much like her sister, Anne resides in Paris where she has worked in the fashion industry most of her adult life. In 1977 she married Jacques Cochin, a son of Baron Denis Cochin and of the former Thérèse de Fréval de Ribains. Anne and Jacques are also the parents of two children: Nicolas and, born in 1979, and Dorothée, born in 1985.

The only son and heir Prince Carlo was born Saint-Raphäel in February 1963. He received the title of Duke of Calabria from his father, who was by then using the title of Duke of Castro as claimant to the throne. Prince Carlo completed his studies at the Institute of the Marist Fathers in Toulon, at the Collège Stanislas in Nice and later studied at the Université Internationale Libre in Paris. In 2008, after his father's death, the Duke of Calabria assumed the title of Duke of Castro as Head of House Two Sicilies.

Opposite page: Prince Carlo and Princess Camilla, then Duke and Duchess of Calabria.

Prince Carlo lived in New York City several years, while he worked

The Duke and Duchess of Castro.

Left: The Duke of Castro and his son Prince Carlo, Duke of Calabria.

Above: The Duke of Calabria, the Duchess of Castro, Luciano Pavarotti and the Duke of Castro.

Below left: The Duke of Castro visiting Naples, former capital of the the Kingdom of the Two Sicilies, along with members of his family.

Below: The Duke of Castro with one of his supporters.

there for a major public relations firm. Upon his return to Europe, Prince Carlo worked for several important Italian enterprises. One of them included a shipbuilding company located in Naples, ancient capital of the kingdom once ruled by his ancestors. He is fluent in Italian, French and English.

On October 31, 1998 Prince Carlo an Italian lady, Camilla Crociani, daughter of a well-known Italian industrialist, Camillo Crociani and of his wife, the former Edoarda Vesselovsky. Due to her father's multiple business affairs, Camilla lived for several years in Mexico and in the United States, where she attended a private Catholic school before attending New York University. Since her father died unexpectedly in 1980, Camilla inherited a considerable fortune with interests

The Duke of Castro and the Duke of Calabria.

A view of the wedding ceremony of Prince Carlo and Princess Camilla. To her left is Prince Laurent of Belgium. To Carlo's right are Prince Rainier III and Hereditary Prince Albert of Monaco.

Top left: The Duke of Castro escorting his daughter Princess Anne.

Top Right: Princess Anne and Princess Beatrice in Paris.

Left, center: At the wedding of Princess Anne, the Dukes of Castro, the Countess of Barcelona, the Duke of Calabria and Princess Beatrice. Behind them are, among others: Prince Giovanni, Princess Elisabeth and Prince Antonio of Bourbon-Two Sicilies.

Left bottom: Princess Anne of Bourbon-Two Sicilies and the Dukes d'Anjou, Prince Charles-Philippe and Diana d'Orléans.

Bottom: The Duke and Duchess of Calabria greeting well-wishers after their wedding.

The Duke and Duchess of Calabria.

worldwide. She is also a polyglot and is fluent in at least five languages: Italian, English, French, Spanish and Japanese. Before her marriage, Camilla was also a recognized equestrian. Today, the Duchess of Castro is very active in the promotion of the charitable, humanitarian and inter-religious activities of the Constantinian Order in Italy and across the world.

Carlos and Camilla's wedding ceremony was celebrated in Monaco in October 1998. Among the bevy of royalty present were Prince Rainier III and Hereditary Prince Albert of Monaco, as well as Prince Laurent of Belgium. The Duke of Castro escorted his daughter-in-law since her father had sadly passed away. From the marriage two daughters were born: Princess Maria Carolina, Duchess of Palermo, born in 2003, and Princess Maria Chiara, Duchess of Capri, born two years later – both born in Rome, where the family has one of their various homes.

As Grand Master of the Sacred Military Constantinian Order of St. George he promotes and coordinates the humanitarian and cultural activities of this ancient knightly order.

An avid hunter, the Duke of Castro is regularly seen attending major hunts organized by royals across the

The Dukes of Calabria attending Monaco's Rose Ball in 2000.

The Dukes of Calabria with their daughters, Maria Carolina and Maria Chiara, attending a royal baptism in Denmark.

European continent. He has been present at several major royal events: the wedding of Crown Prince Frederik of Denmark (he is the godfather of one of the Danish Crown Princely couple's children), the swearing-in of Prince Albert II of Monaco, as well as his wedding, the wedding of Prince Laurent of Belgium, and many others.

The Duchess of Castro has always supported charity associations, including UNICEF and the Red Cross, and she is an active public figure, which promotes the arts, culture and sport of southern Italy. The Duchess of Castro also plays a prominent role in the national and international activities of the dynastic orders of the Royal House of Bourbon Two Sicilies especially those that relate to charitable and humanitarian assistance.

Opposite page:
Prince Carlo and
Princess Camilla, Duke
and Duchess of Castro.

The Duchess of Castro.

Top left: The Duke of Castro with Princess Chantal of Bourbon-Parma

Top right: The Duchess of Castro with Prince Charles Emmanuel of Bourbon-Parma.

Left: The Duke of Castro at the Vatican, October 2004.

Below: The Dukes of Castro in Potsdam attending the wedding of Prince Georg Friedrich of Prussia and Princess Sophie of Isenburg.

Top left: The Duke and Duchess of Castro in Monaco, 2005.

Top right: The Dukes of Castro at Queen Fabiola of Belgium's funeral.

Below: Princess Maria Chiara, the Duchess of Bragança, the Prince of Beira, the Duke of Oporto, Princess Maria Carolina and the Duchess of Castro, Portugal 2014.

Below bottom: The Duke of Castro and Prince Leka of Albania.

Below right: The Duke of Noto and the Duke of Castro after signing the Act of Family Reconciliation, Naples, 2014.

CHAPTER XIV
Filippo

rince Filippo was born at the Villa Marie Thérèse in Cannes on December 10, 1885. He was the Casertas' tenth child and sixth son. As was the case with his siblings, the tutors and nannies his parents had employed to instruct their older children first educated him at home. Several of these servants were none other than old Sicilian nobility who served their exiled royal family with great abnegation and loyalty.

When it came time for Filippo to begin building a future career, he also attended the Spanish Military Academy for Cavalry and like his brothers obtained a commission.

In 1916 he made a grand marriage to Princess Marie-Louise of Orléans, daughter of Prince Emmanuel, Duke of Vendôme, by his wife Princess Henriette of Belgium. Marie-Louise, who was born at Neuilly-sur-Seine on December 31, 1896. Just five months later her father lost his mother, the Duchess d'Alençon, a sister of Queen Maria Sophia of the Two Sicilies, in a tragic fire that consumed a Parisian bazaar where she had been selling items for charity. Marie-Louise's grandfather, the devastated Duke d'Alençon, Prince Ferdinand d'Orléans, was the only brother of the Count d'Eu, father-in-law of Princess Maria Pia of the Bourbon-Two Sicilies, Prince Filippo's sister. The family of the Duke de Vendôme divided its time between the Parisian residence and the Château de Tourronde, a beautiful estate on Lake Leman just a few miles away of Evian, that the Duchess de Vendôme had purchased with the inheritance she received from her parents' considerable fortune. Princess Henriette of Belgium

Prince Filippo of Bourbon-Two Sicilies.

(1870-1948) was one of the children of the Count of Flanders, brother of King Leopold II of the Belgians. She was, therefore, a sister of King Albert I of the Belgians. Besides their daughter Marie-Louise, the Vendômes had three other younger children Sophie (1898-1928), who was handicapped; Geneviève (1901-1983), who married Antoine, Marquis de Chaponay; and Charles Philippe (1905-1970), Duke de Nemours, who married American Marguerite Watson.

Opposite page: Prince Filippo of Bourbon-Two Sicilies.

Prince Filippo and Princess Marie-Louise's wedding took place at Neuilly-sur-Seine, on the outskirts of Paris, and in spite of the war raging along the Western Front, was attended by several

The Dukes de Vendôme with their daughters: Marie-Louise, Sophie and Génevive d'Orléans.

The Duchess de Vendôme and her daughter Princess Marie-Louise.

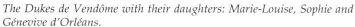

members of other European Royal Houses, many of them living in wartime Paris. Although a son, Gaetano, was born in 1917 the marriage did not last, as the couple were incompatible. In due time, they separated and divorced, with a subsequent annulment granted by the Catholic Church in 1926.

Marie-Louise went on to remarry a wealthy American named Walter Kingsland. The couple traveled extensively and eventually settled in the United States. Mr. Kingsland died in New York in 1961, while Princess Marie-Louise passed away there in March 1973.

Prince Filippo also married again in 1927 a French woman called Odette Labori, who was a well-known early woman tennis player. As Odette's previous brief marriage had also been annulled the old Count of Caserta had to accept her marriage to Filippo as legally valid, and gradually Odette became accepted by the family and was invited to all the great gatherings in Cannes.

During the Second World War Odette served as

Opposite page: Prince Filippo of Bourbon-Two Sicilies and his first wife, Princess Marie-Louise d'Orléans.

Princess Marie-Louise d'Orléans.

a Red Cross Nurse and was also a member of the French resistance. After the war was over she was invited by various groups in French-speaking Canada to go over and lecture about her experiences. On a visit in 1949 Prince Filippo fell seriously ill with pneumonia ill and died in the town of St. John in the province of New Brunswick. His widow Odette lived in Paris in a state of complete penury and had to be financially assisted by several of her husband's relatives until her death. Odette passed away at Le Kremlin-Bicetre in June 1968.

Prince Gaetano, his only son, was awarded to his father when his parents split up, and spent a rather gloomy childhood, consigned to English nannies and boarding school, enlivened only by visits to his ageing grandparents in Cannes. From time to time, Prince Gaetano spent short periods with his maternal family mainly at the Château de Tourronde, where his artistic and politically active Belgian grandmother continued living after the early death of the Duke de Vendôme in 1931, who died of a heart failure after catching a cold in Cannes.

Prince Gaetano decided to stay in England, where his mother and Mr. Kingsland had lived for some time. In 1938 was working as an engineer at Runcorn, an industrial town and port in Cheshire. Early in 1939, he became a naturalized British citizen and several months later renounced his rights of succession to the throne of the Two Sicilies. At

Prince Filippo and Princess Marie-Louise of Bourbon-Two Sicilies.

Prince Filippo and Princess Marie-Louise.

Prince Filippo in Spanish military uniform.

Princess Marie-Louise and baby Prince Gaetano.

Odette Labori, second wife of Prince Filippo.

the outbreak of the Second World War he joined the war effort as plain Mr. de Bourbon. He served as an officer with the Royal Navy until the end of the war.

In 1946, in London, he married Olivia Yarrow, daughter of Lt. Commander Charles Yarrow. The couple decided to seek their fortunes in Africa and immigrated firstly to Kenya, then to Rhodesia (now Zimbabwe) where they settled and remained for the rest of their lives and where two sons, Adrian and Gregory were born to them in 1948 and 1950 respectively. Gaetano died at Harare in 1984, while Olivia survived him three years, dying also at Harare in 1987. Gaetano, former Prince of Bourbon-Two Sicilies was the only one of the three grandchildren of the Dukes de Vendôme to leave descendants as his de Chaponay cousins were childless, one dying during the Second World War, while the other remained unmarried.

Adrian de Bourbon became a well know and successful advocate in Zimbabwe, but due to difficult political conditions moved to South Africa. In 1976 he married Linda Rose Idensohn (b. 1950) and by her had two children: Philippe Charles (b. 1977) and Michelle Laura (b. 1979), both now married. In 1994, the Duke of Castro granted "ad personam" to Adrian and his brother Gregory the title of "Prince of Bourbon."

The Duke de Vendôme.

The Duke de Nemours with his nephew Prince Gaetano of Bourbon-Two Sicilies.

Princess Marie-Louise d'Orléans, Mrs. Kingsland.

Prince Gaetano of Bourbon-Two Sicilies.

Marie-Louise and Charles Philippe with their mother Henriette.

The Duchess de Vendôme.

This image was taken at the wedding of Princess Génevieve d'Orléans and the Marquis de Chaponay. Princess Génevieve is surrounded by the bridal children. The boy to the right of the image is her nephew Prince Gaetano of Bourbon-Two Sicilies.

Prince Gaetano and his wife, Ms. Olivia Yarrow

Gregory, Adrian's youngest and only brother, now lives in Australia. He married firstly Maureen Marjorie Powell (b. 1951) and by her had two sons: Christian Peter (b. 1974) and Raymond (b. 1978). The first of the children was born in Vancouver, Canada, while the couple's youngest was born in Harare. Both are married and have children.

Prince Gregory of Bourbon married secondly in Queensland, Australia, Carrie-Ann Thornley (b. 1945). They have traveled several times to Europe and met with some of his Bourbon-Two Sicilies relations.

Above: Prince Adrian de Bourbon.

Right top: Prince Gregory de Bourbon.

Right below: Prince Gregory and Princess Carrie-Ann de Bourbon.

Below: Prince Gregory and Princess Carrie-Ann de Bourbon with Princess Dolores of Bourbon-Two Sicilies.

Below bottom: Prince Adrian de Bourbon.

CHAPTER XV

Gabriele

Known in the family by his nickname "Onga," Prince Gabriele, the benjamin of the family was born in 1897, when his oldest sibling Ferdinando was almost twenty-eight-years old and about to become a father.

Another favorite in the Spanish Royal Household, Prince Gabriele was accorded Spanish nationality by King Alfonso in 1920 with the title "Príncipe de Borbón" and the style of Royal Highness. As a sign of the high regard King Alfonso XIII held his Sicilian cousin, Prince Gabriele received the Golden Fleece, an amazing honor.

In 1927, in Paris, he married for the first time. His bride was Princess Malgorzata (Margarita) Czartoryska of the immensely wealthy and influential Polish Princely family, and whose grandmother was Princess Marguerite d'Orléans. Marguerite was a sister of the Count d'Eu and the Duke d'Alençon, their parents being the Duke de Nemours and his wife, the former Princess Victoire of Saxe-Coburg & Gotha, a first cousin of Queen Victoria, as well as one of her closest friends. Coincidentally, as intricate family connections are of interest to us, Malgorzata's father, Fürst Adam Czartoryski, was a first cousin of the Duke de Vendôme, one-tim father-in-law of Prince Filippo of Bourbon-Two Sicilies, Prince Gabriele's brother.

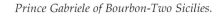

Prince Gabriele of Bourbon-Two Sicilies.

A son Antonio was born to them in January 1929 but Princess Margarita did not recover from the birth and died a few weeks later. The half-orphaned baby Prince was consigned to his paternal grandparents the Casertas in Cannes and remained there until his father married again in 1932 another Polish Princess, Cecilia Lubomirska. She was the daughter of Prince Kasimir Lubomirski (1869-1930), a former ambassador, and of his wife Countess Therese Granow-Wodzicka (1883-1948). The Lubomirskis have featured prominently in Polish history for several

centuries, going back to medieval times. Much like the Radziwills and Czartoryskis, the Lubomirski princes were also great landowners and their estates covered a considerable expanse of territory in what later became Ukraine and Slovakia. All these properties, of course, were lost after the Soviet Union took over Poland and Czechoslovakia in 1945. The Lubomirskis managed to leave Poland as the Russians flooded into the country. In exile, as was the case with everyone coming from Eastern Europe, they had to rebuild their lives. More recently, and since 2010, *"family members have established the Princes Lubomirski Foundation (Polish Fundacja Książąt Lubomirskich), to express and develop charitable activities. The foundation supports the development of various social and heritage projects in Poland."*

Anyhow, by the time Gabriele married Princess Cecilia the Republic had been proclaimed in Spain, putting an end to the Prince's army career. Jobless and with no incentive to return to Spain, he decided to stay in Poland where he occupied himself with the administration of some of the Lubomirski estates. Four

The wedding of Prince Gabriele of Bourbon-Two Sicilies and Princess Malgorzata Czartoryska.

children were born to them in Warsaw and Prince Antonio was returned to his father. Princess Cecilia raised her stepson as her own child and the children grew to be very attached to one another. Her children included: Giovanni (1933-2000), who was unmarried and childless; Maria Margarita (1934-2014), who married Luis Gonzaga Maldonado y Gordon (b. 1932); Maria Immaculata (b. 1937), who was married to Miguel García de Saéz, from whom she divorced in 1979; and Casimiro (b. 1938), who in 1967 married Princess Maria Cristina of Savoy-Aosta (b. 1933).

Opposite page: Prince Gabriele of Bourbon-Two Siciliies and his second bride, Princess Cecilia Lubomirska.

The Second World War put paid to the Polish chapter in Gabriele's life, as everything was lost

Gabriel
Madrid 16 – IV – 1924

Prince Gabriele of Bourbon-Two Sicilies.

to the Communists and the family was forced to flee. They decided to leave Europe and to seek a new life in South America, settling in Southern Brazil, where they acquired an agricultural plantation and where they were especially close to their nephew Prince Pedro Henrique and his family. Prince Gabriele never returned to Europe although his wife did for family events. Prince Gabriele died at Itu, São Paulo, in October 1975, just weeks before the return of the monarchy to Spain in the person of his great-nephew King Juan Carlos I. This was a historical event that would have brought him untold joy since Gabriele, as was the case with his brothers, was a close friend of King Alfonso XIII. Princess Cecilia lived to her mid-nineties and died in São Paulo in September 2001.

Prince Antonio made it to the West with his father and the rest of the family. In due course, he attended university in the United States and obtained a degree in engineering. This was to be his career and he worked successfully in Europe. In July 1958, Antonio married at Schloß Altshausen Duchess Elisabeth of Württemberg (b. 1933), daughter of the Head of the family, Duke Philipp-Albrecht and of his second wife, the former Archduchess Rosa of

Prince Gabriele of Bourbon-Two Sicilies.

In Brazil: Prince Gabriele with his great-nephew Prince Bertrand d'Orléans-Bragança.

The wedding of Prince Antonio of Bourbon-Two Sicilies and Duchess Elisabeth of Württemberg. From the left: Prince Giovanni of Bourbon-Two Sicilies, Princess Marie Christine and Prince Georg of Liechtenstein, the Duchess of Württemberg, the newlyweds, the Duke of Württemberg and Princess Cecilia of Bourbon-Two Sicilies.

Austria-Tuscany. Readers will recall that Elisabeth shares several Bourbon-Two Sicilies connections with her husband. Her maternal grandmother was born Princess Maria Christina of Bourbon-Two Sicilies, one of the four daughters of the Counts of Caserta, and thus a sister of Gabriele, Elisabeth's father-in-law. Also, as a descendant of Queen Marie Amelie of the French, Elisabeth also descends from King Ferdinando I and Queen Maria Carolina.

Prince Antonio and Princess Elisabeth, who remain very close to her siblings, are frequent guests at various gatherings in Schloß Altshausen and Schloß Friedrichshafen. He is now retired after a long career as an engineer and they reside in Lausanne, Switzerland.

The couple had four children: Francesco (b. 1960), who in 2000 married Countess Alexandra von Schönborn-Wiesentheid (b. 1967), daughter of Count Franz Clemens and of his first wife, Princess Tatjana Gortschakow; Maria Carolina (b. 1962), who in 1989 married Andreas Baumbach (b. 1963); Gennaro (b. 1966), unmarried; and Maria Annunziata (b. 1973), who in 2003 married in Helsinki, Finland, Count Carl Fredrik Creutz (b. 1971).

Of the four children of Prince Gabriele's second marriage, the elder son Prince Giovanni was unmarried, as mentioned before. He died on Christmas day in 2000 after a long illness that caused him great discomfort. Painful sessions of chemotherapy did not succeed in helping him defeat the cancer of the spine that caused him such misery, which he bore with Christian fortitude and resignation. *"It is nothing,"* he told our friend Ricardo Mateos Sainz de Medrano, *"that's life and*

Prince Antonio and Princess Elisabeth of Bourbon-Two Sicilies.

Schloß Altshausen, July 1960 – Wedding of Duke Carl of Württemberg and Princess Diane of France. Standing in back, from left: Princess Claude of France; Duchess Helene and Duchess Marie Antoinette of Württemberg; Prince Michael of Greece; Princess Hélène of France, Countess Limburg Stirum; Prince François, Princess Anne, Prince Michel and Princess Isabelle of France; Count Evrard de Limburg Stirum; Prince Jacques of France; Princess Elisabeth and Prince Antonio of Bourbon-Two Sicilies; Princess Marie Christine of Liechtenstein; the Count de Clermont. Seated, same order: The Duke of Württemberg; the Countess of Paris; the Duchess of Württemberg; Duke Carl and Duchess Diane of Württemberg; the Count of Paris; and the Countess de Clermont. Seated on the floor are: Prince Thibaut and Princess Chantal of France.

we have to face it the best way."

Prince Giovanni was keenly interested in history, particularly that of his dynasty. One of his last joys was a journey to Naples that he accomplished just before his death.

He was also quite popular among the Gotha and the Countess of Barcelona relished visiting with Prince Giovanni, her first cousin. Interestingly, in spite of the rift that pitted her brother and nephew against other members of the dynasty, doña María always enjoyed excellent relations with all her Bourbon-Two Sicilies cousins. The Duke and Duchess of Württemberg, Carl and Diane, thought so highly of him that he was chosen

Schloß Altshausen, 1966. From left: Duke Friedrich of Württemberg, Princess Marie of France, the Count of Paris and Prince Francesco of Bourbon-Two Sicilies.

Top left: Duke Carl and Duchess Diane of Württemberg, Prince Antonio of Bourbon-Two Sicilies and Princess Marie Christine of Liechtenstein.

Top right: Prince Giovanni of Bourbon-Two Sicilies and Duchess Diane of Württemberg.

Left: Prince Antonio, Prince Giovanni, Princess Maria Margherita, Princess Maria Immaculata, Prince Casimiro.

Below: Princess Elisabeth of Bourbon-Two Sicilies, Duke Carl of Württemberg, the Duchess de Montpensier.

Bottom left: Princess Marie Christine of Liechtenstein, Prince Antonio and Princess Elisabeth of Bourbon-Two Sicilies.

Bottom right: Prince Antonio of Bourbon-Two Sicilies and his nephew the Duke de Vendôme.

as the godfather of their eldest daughter, Duchess Mathilde, who frequently invited Giovanni to come visit her in Germany. Being closer in age to the Countess of Barcelona's children, Giovanni was also close to King Juan Carlos and his sisters. Ricardo Mateos once recalled an interesting snapshot Prince Giovanni showed him, *"at his tiny but beautifully furnished and decorated flat in Madrid showing himself wearing a fleur-de-lys apron and holding arm in arm the King and Queen for whom he had cooked a special dinner that night."*

Prince Giovanni had exquisite manners and was highly educated. He possessed great knowledge about art, history, genealogy, royalty and cuisine, even having a book of recipes published just before his death. He worked for Spanish Vogue in Madrid, and had already worked several years in Paris for an important couture house. This erudite prince was also an exceptional conversationalist and recognized linguist as he was able to fluently converse in Italian, polish, Portuguese, French, English, German and Spanish, which he spoke *"with a sweet touch of Italian accent."*

Prince Antonio and Princess Elisabeth of Bourbon-Two Sicilies, Altshausen, August 2003.

In accordance to the prince's wishes, he was cremated and his ashes were transported to Naples and buried there.

As mentioned earlier, Prince Gabriele and Princess Cecilia's youngest son, Prince Casimiro, married Princess Maria Christina of Savoy. She is the daughter of Prince Amedeo of Savoy (1898-1942), 3rd Duke of Aosta, and of

From left; Princess Elisabeth, (?), Princess Maria Immaculata, Prince Giovanni, Prince Antonio, Princess Maria Margarita, and don Luis Gonzaga Maldonado y Gordon.

his French wife, Princess Anne (1906-1986), the third daughter of the Duke and Duchess de Guise. Anne's father became Head of House France in 1926 and her brother, Henri, Count of Paris, succeeded their father in that position in 1940. Furthermore, Maria Christina is also the first cousin of Prince Michael of Greece, himself a close friend of his cousin Queen Sofia of Spain, as he was the only son of Princess Françoise of France and her husband Prince Christopher of Greece, an uncle of the Duke of Edinburgh, husband of HM Queen Elizabeth II.

The 3rd Duke of Aosta was a respected and admired soldier who enjoyed a prestigious career in

Opposite page: Prince Giovanni of Bourbon-Two Sicilies.

La luz de su rostro al morir reflejaba la paz de su alma.

Anima Christi, santífica me
Corpus Christi, salva me
Sanguis Christi, inébra me
Aqua láteris Christi, lava me
Pássio Christi, confórta me
O bone Jesu, exáudi me
Intra tua vúlnera, abscónde me
Ne permíttas me separári a te
Ab hoste malígno, defénde me
In hora mortis meae, voca me
Et jube me venire ad te
Ut cum Sanctis tuis laudem
In saecula saeculórum

Amen.

Sainte Vierge de Czestochowa, priez pour moi !

Santo Anjo do Senhor, nosso zeloso guardador
Já que á vós, vos confiou a piedade divina,
Sempre nos reje, guarda, governa e ilumina

Amen.

RICORDATEVI NELLE VOSTRE PREGHIERE
DI
SUA ALTEZZA REALE
GIOVANNI DI BORBONE
PRINCIPE DELLE DUE SICILIE

NATO A VARSOVIA IL 30 GIUGNO 1933
PIAMENTE ADDORMENTATO NEL SIGNORE
A MADRID IL 24 DICEMBRE 2000

Death card of Prince Giovanni of Bourbon-Two Sicilies.

Italy's military. Amedeo and his family lived in the beautiful and historical Castle of Miramare, near Trieste. In fact, they were to be Miramare's last royal occupants as the Savoys lost the property after

Top left: Wedding of Princess Maria Immaculata and Miguel García de Saez.

Top right: Prince Giovanni, Princess Maria Margarita, Princess Elisabeth and Prince Antonio.

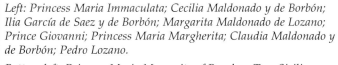

Left: Princess Maria Immaculata; Cecilia Maldonado y de Borbón; Ilia García de Saez y de Borbón; Margarita Maldonado de Lozano; Prince Giovanni; Princess Maria Margherita; Claudia Maldonado y de Borbón; Pedro Lozano.

Bottom left: Princess Maria Margarita of Bourbon-Two Sicilies.

Bottom right: Miguel García de Saez, Princess Maria Immaculata and the Dukes of Badajoz: Infanta Pilar of Spain and Luis Gómez-Acebo.

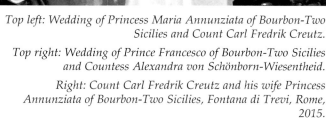

Top left: Wedding of Princess Maria Annunziata of Bourbon-Two Sicilies and Count Carl Fredrik Creutz.

Top right: Wedding of Prince Francesco of Bourbon-Two Sicilies and Countess Alexandra von Schönborn-Wiesentheid.

Right: Count Carl Fredrik Creutz and his wife Princess Annunziata of Bourbon-Two Sicilies, Fontana di Trevi, Rome, 2015.

Bottom: Prince Francesco and Princess Alexandra of Bourbon-Two Sicilies with the princess's mother, Princess Tatjana Gortschakow.

the fall of the monarchy in June 1946. The Dukes of Aosta also had an older daughter, Margherita, who married Archduke Robert, the second son of Emperor Karl and Empress Zita of Austria. This connection has given Casimiro and Maria Christina a close link to the Belgian royal court since she is the aunt of Archduke Lorenz, husband of Princess Astrid of Belgium, only daughter of former King Albert II. Another nephew of Princess Maria Christina is Archduke Martin of Austria, who in 2004 married Princess Katharina of Isenburg, a wedding well-attended by various members of the Bourbon-Two Sicilies Royal Family. Katharina's sisters also married rather illustriously: Isabelle is the widow of the Fürst of Wied, while Sophie is the wife of Prince Georg Friedrich of Prussia.

Sadly, Maria Christina and Margherita lost their father early. In the late 1930s Amedeo, who was already a brilliant aviator, was sent to serve as Vice-Roy of Ethiopia and Governor-General of the Italian provinces in Eastern Africa. He was still serving in this position when the Allies defeated the Italians in that part of Africa during the Second World War. Amedeo, who fought valiantly and was extremely well-respected, even by his opponents, refused any special treatment and was detained in a prisoner of war camp near Nairobi, Kenya. Unfortunately, while there he contracted typhus and died on March 3, 1942.

The Widowed Duchess of Aosta had a difficult time in the postwar era. Destruction surrounded her and the family was now dethroned and facing challenging financial times. Yet, she did not balk at the

Prince Casimiro of Bourbon-Two Sicilies and Princess Margherita of Savoy.

Prince Casimiro and Princess Maria Christina of Bourbon-Two Sicilies at the funeral of the Countess of Paris, Dreux, 2003.

Prince Casimiro of Bourbon-Two Sicilies, Rome, 2004.

troubles facing her and focus on rebuilding their life. Aided by an improving financial situation, particularly by the inheritance she received from her father the Duke de Guise (who had died in Morocco during the war), Anne of Aosta was able to provide her daughters with a solid foundation and a loving environment. She remained very close to her siblings, particularly the Count of Paris, who acted as "pater familias" for the extended family. The Widowed Duchess of Aosta died in Sorrento, Italy, 1986, a few months short of her eightieth birthday. Her passing was a great loss to her daughters, sons-in-law and many grandchildren.

Prince Luis Alfonso of Bourbon-Two Sicilies.

Prince Casimiro and Princess Maria Christina, who also had many ties with Brazil, married in the private chapel of the bishop of Jacarezinho, in the Brazilian state of Paraná. The wedding took place in January 1967. The couple settled in Brazil and it was there that their four children were born: Luis Alfonso (b. 1970), who firstly married Christine Apovian (b. 1969), by whom he has a daughter (Anna), and married secondly Maria da Glória Ganem Rubião, by whom he has three children (Maria Isabel, Luisa Fernanda and Paulo Alfonso); Anna Cecilia (b. 1971), who married Count Rodolphe de Vincens de Causans (b. 1973); Elena Sofia (b. 1973); and Alessandro (b. 1974), who was ordained as a Catholic priest in 2007.

Left, top: Princess Elena of Bourbon-Two Sicilies.

Left middle: The wedding of Princess Anna Cecilia of Bourbon-Two Sicilies and Count Rodolphe de Vincens de Causans.

Left: Father Alessandro (né Prince Alessandro of Bourbon-Two Sicilies).

In spite of their deep roots in the Old World, Prince Casimiro and Princess Maria Christina continue to live in Brazil, but return frequently to Europe for family events.

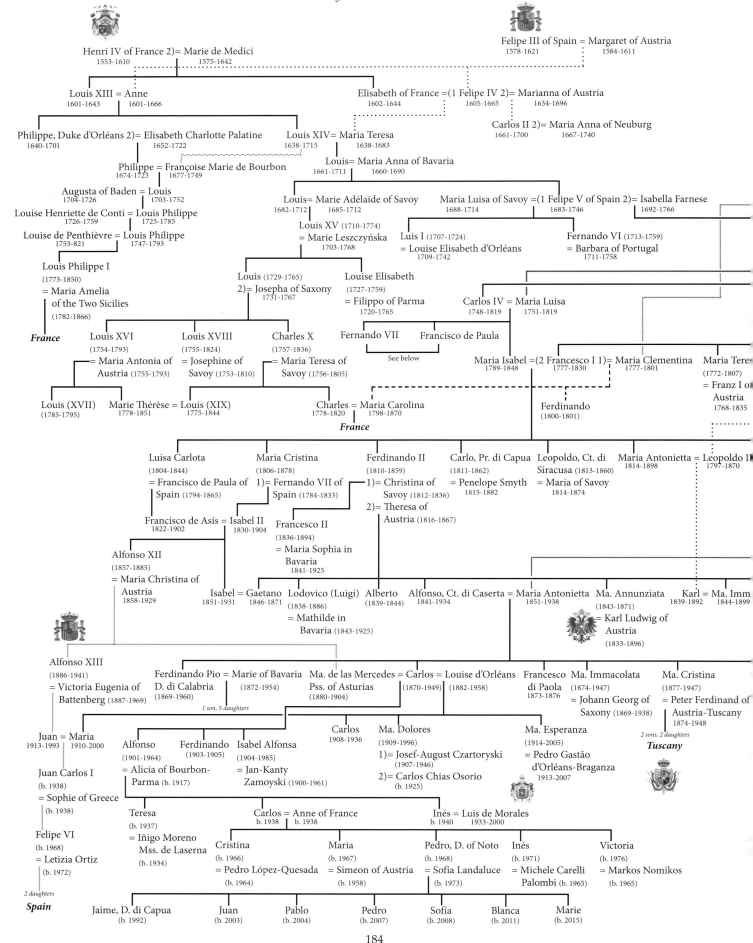

Henri IV of France 2)= Marie de Medici
1553-1610 1575-1642

Felipe III of Spain = Margaret of Austria
1578-1621 1584-1611

Louis XIII = Anne
1601-1643 1601-1666

Elisabeth of France =(1 Felipe IV 2)= Marianna of Austria
1602-1644 1605-1665 1634-1696

Carlos II 2)= Maria Anna of Neuburg
1661-1700 1667-1740

Philippe, Duke d'Orléans 2)= Elisabeth Charlotte Palatine
1640-1701 1652-1722

Louis XIV= Maria Teresa
1638-1715 1638-1683

Louis= Maria Anna of Bavaria
1661-1711 1660-1690

Philippe = Françoise Marie de Bourbon
1674-1723 1677-1749

Louis= Marie Adélaïde of Savoy
1682-1712 1685-1712

Maria Luisa of Savoy =(1 Felipe V of Spain 2)= Isabella Farnese
1688-1714 1683-1746 1692-1766

Augusta of Baden = Louis
1704-1726 1703-1752

Louis XV (1710-1774)
= Marie Leszczyńska
1703-1768

Luis I (1707-1724)
= Louise Elisabeth d'Orléans
1709-1742

Fernando VI (1713-1759)
= Barbara of Portugal
1711-1758

Louise Henriette de Conti = Louis Philippe
1726-1759 1725-1785

Louise de Penthièvre = Louis Philippe
1753-821 1747-1793

Louis (1729-1765)
2)= Josepha of Saxony
1731-1767

Louise Elisabeth (1727-1759)
= Filippo of Parma
1720-1765

Carlos IV = Maria Luisa
1748-1819 1751-1819

Louis Philippe I (1773-1850)
= Maria Amelia
of the Two Sicilies
(1782-1866)

France

Louis XVI (1754-1793)
= Maria Antonia of
Austria (1755-1793)

Louis XVIII (1755-1824)
= Josephine of
Savoy (1753-1810)

Charles X (1757-1836)
= Maria Teresa of
Savoy (1756-1805)

Fernando VII Francisco de Paula
See below

Maria Isabel =(2 Francesco I 1)= Maria Clementina
1789-1848 1777-1830 1777-1801

Maria Teres
(1772-1807)
= Franz I o
Austria
1768-1835

Louis (XVII) (1785-1795)

Marie Thérèse = Louis (XIX)
1778-1851 1775-1844

Charles = Maria Carolina
1778-1820 1798-1870

Ferdinando (1800-1801)

France

Luisa Carlota (1804-1844)
= Francisco de Paula of
Spain (1794-1865)

Maria Cristina (1806-1878)
1)= Fernando VII of
Spain (1784-1833)

Ferdinando II (1810-1859)
1)= Christina of
Savoy (1812-1836)
2)= Theresa of
Austria (1816-1867)

Carlo, Pr. di Capua (1811-1862)
= Penelope Smyth
1815-1882

Leopoldo, Ct. di
Siracusa (1813-1860)
= Maria of Savoy
1814-1874

Maria Antonietta = Leopoldo I
1814-1898 1797-1870

Francisco de Asís = Isabel II
1822-1902 1830-1904

Francesco II (1836-1894)
= Maria Sophia in
Bavaria
1841-1925

Alfonso XII (1857-1885)
= Maria Christina of
Austria
1858-1929

Isabel = Gaetano
1851-1931 1846-1871

Lodovico (Luigi) (1838-1886)
= Mathilde in
Bavaria (1843-1925)

Alberto (1839-1844)

Alfonso, Ct. di Caserta = Maria Antonietta
1841-1934 1851-1938

Ma. Annunziata (1843-1871)
= Karl Ludwig of
Austria (1833-1896)

Karl = Ma. Imm
1839-1892 1844-1899

Alfonso XIII (1886-1941)
= Victoria Eugenia of
Battenberg (1887-1969)

Ferdinando Pio = Marie of Bavaria
D. di Calabria (1872-1954)
(1869-1960)
1 son, 5 daughters

Ma. de las Mercedes = Carlos = Louise d'Orléans
Pss. of Asturias (1870-1949) (1882-1958)
(1880-1904)

Francesco
di Paola
1873-1876

Ma. Immacolata (1874-1947)
= Johann Georg of
Saxony (1869-1938)

Ma. Cristina (1877-1947)
= Peter Ferdinand of
Austria-Tuscany
1874-1948

Juan = Maria
1913-1993 1910-2000

Alfonso (1901-1964)
= Alicia of Bourbon-
Parma (b. 1917)

Ferdinando (1903-1905)

Isabel Alfonsa (1904-1985)
= Jan-Kanty
Zamoyski (1900-1961)

Carlos 1908-1936

Ma. Dolores (1909-1996)
1)= Josef-August Czartoryski
(1907-1946)
2)= Carlos Chias Osorio
(b. 1925)

Ma. Esperanza (1914-2005)
= Pedro Gastão
d'Orléans-Braganza
1913-2007

2 sons, 2 daughters

Tuscany

Juan Carlos I (b. 1938)
= Sophie of Greece
(b. 1938)

Teresa (b. 1937)
= Iñigo Moreno
Mss. de Laserna
(b. 1934)

Carlos = Anne of France
b. 1938 b. 1938

Inés = Luis de Morales
b. 1940 1933-2000

Felipe VI (b. 1968)
= Letizia Ortiz
(b. 1972)

Cristina (b. 1966)
= Pedro López-Quesada
(b. 1964)

Maria (b. 1967)
= Simeon of Austria
(b. 1958)

Pedro, D. of Noto (b. 1968)
= Sofía Landaluce
(b. 1973)

Inés (b. 1971)
= Michele Carelli
Palombi (b. 1965)

Victoria (b. 1976)
= Markos Nomikos
(b. 1965)

2 daughters

Spain

Jaime, D. di Capua (b. 1992)
Juan (b. 2003)
Pablo (b. 2004)
Pedro (b. 2007)
Sofía (b. 2008)
Blanca (b. 2011)
Marie (b. 2015)

The Royal Family of the Two Sicilies

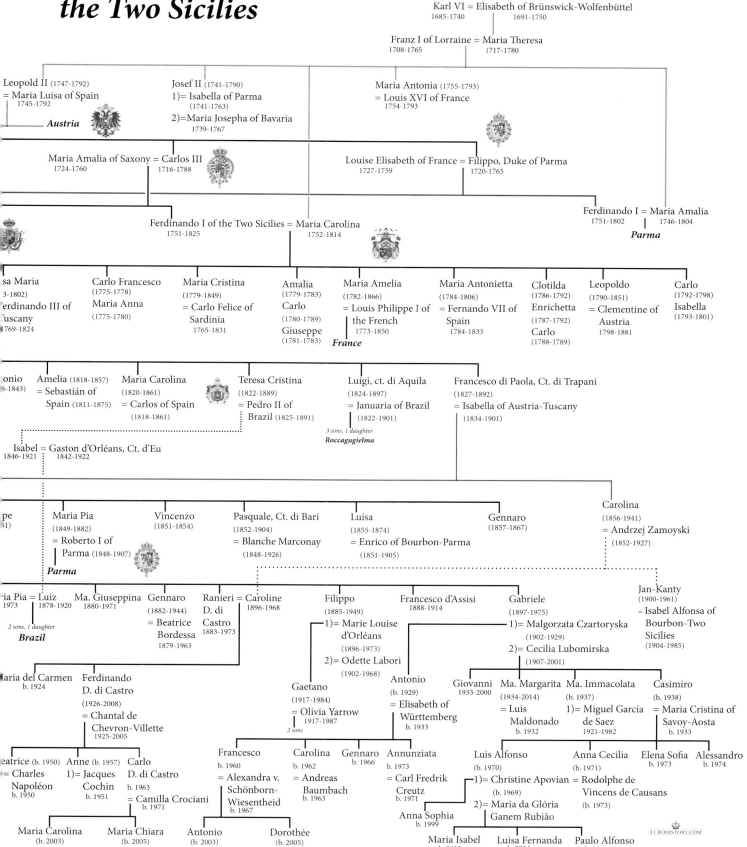

Karl VI = Elisabeth of Brünswick-Wolfenbüttel
1685-1740   1691-1750

Franz I of Lorraine = Maria Theresa
1708-1765   1717-1780

Leopold II (1747-1792)
= Maria Luisa of Spain
1745-1792
Austria

Josef II (1741-1790)
1)= Isabella of Parma
(1741-1763)
2)=Maria Josepha of Bavaria
1739-1767

Maria Antonia (1755-1793)
= Louis XVI of France
1754-1793

Maria Amalia of Saxony = Carlos III
1724-1760   1716-1788

Louise Elisabeth of France = Filippo, Duke of Parma
1727-1759   1720-1765

Ferdinando I = Maria Amalia
1751-1802   1746-1804
Parma

Ferdinando I of the Two Sicilies = Maria Carolina
1751-1825   1752-1814

...sa Maria
(3-1802)
...rdinando III of
...uscany
...1769-1824

Carlo Francesco
(1775-1778)
Maria Anna
(1775-1780)

Maria Cristina
(1779-1849)
= Carlo Felice of
Sardinia
1765-1831

Amalia
(1779-1783)
Carlo
(1780-1789)
Giuseppe
(1781-1783)
France

Maria Amelia
(1782-1866)
= Louis Philippe I of
the French
1773-1850

Maria Antonietta
(1784-1806)
= Fernando VII of
Spain
1784-1833

Clotilda
(1786-1792)
Enrichetta
(1787-1792)
Carlo
(1788-1789)

Leopoldo
(1790-1851)
= Clementine of
Austria
1798-1881

Carlo
(1792-1798)
Isabella
(1793-1801)

...onio
...5-1843)

Amelia (1818-1857)
= Sebastián of
Spain (1811-1875)

Maria Carolina
(1820-1861)
= Carlos of Spain
(1818-1861)

Teresa Cristina
(1822-1889)
= Pedro II of
Brazil (1825-1891)

Luigi, ct. di Aquila
(1824-1897)
= Januaria of Brazil
(1822-1901)
3 sons, 1 daughter
Roccagugielma

Francesco di Paola, Ct. di Trapani
(1827-1892)
= Isabella of Austria-Tuscany
(1834-1901)

...Isabel = Gaston d'Orléans, Ct. d'Eu
1846-1921   1842-1922

...pe
...51)

Maria Pia
(1849-1882)
= Roberto I of
Parma (1848-1907)
Parma

Vincenzo
(1851-1854)

Pasquale, Ct. di Bari
(1852-1904)
= Blanche Marconay
(1848-1926)

Luisa
(1855-1874)
= Enrico of Bourbon-Parma
(1851-1905)

Gennaro
(1857-1867)

Carolina
(1856-1941)
= Andrzej Zamoyski
(1852-1927)

...ia Pia = Luiz
...1973   1878-1920
2 sons, 1 daughter
Brazil

Ma. Giuseppina
1880-1971

Gennaro
(1882-1944)
= Beatrice
Bordessa
1879-1963

Ranieri = Caroline
D. di   1896-1968
Castro
1883-1973

Filippo
(1885-1949)
1)= Marie Louise
d'Orléans
(1896-1973)
2)= Odette Labori
(1902-1968)

Francesco d'Assisi
1888-1914

Gabriele
(1897-1975)
1)= Malgorzata Czartoryska
(1902-1929)
2)= Cecilia Lubomirska
(1907-2001)

Jan-Kanty
(1900-1961)
= Isabel Alfonsa of
Bourbon-Two
Sicilies
(1904-1985)

...aria del Carmen
b. 1924

Ferdinando
D. di Castro
(1926-2008)
= Chantal de
Chevron-Villette
1925-2005

Gaetano
(1917-1984)
= Olivia Yarrow
1917-1987
2 sons

Antonio
(b. 1929)
= Elisabeth of
Württemberg
b. 1933

Giovanni
1933-2000

Ma. Margarita
(1934-2014)
= Luis
Maldonado
b. 1932

Ma. Immacolata
(b. 1937)
1)= Miguel García
de Saez
1921-1982

Casimiro
(b. 1938)
= Maria Cristina of
Savoy-Aosta
b. 1933

...eatrice (b. 1950)
= Charles
Napoléon
b. 1950

Anne (b. 1957)
1)= Jacques
Cochin
b. 1951

Carlo
D. di Castro
b. 1963
= Camilla Crociani
b. 1971

Francesco
b. 1960
= Alexandra v.
Schönborn-
Wiesentheid
b. 1967

Carolina
b. 1962
= Andreas
Baumbach
b. 1963

Gennaro
b. 1966

Annunziata
b. 1973
= Carl Fredrik
Creutz
b. 1971

Luis Alfonso
(b. 1970)
1)= Christine Apovian
(b. 1969)
2)= Maria da Glória
Ganem Rubião

Anna Cecilia
(b. 1971)
= Rodolphe de
Vincens de Causans
(b. 1973)

Elena Sofia
b. 1973

Alessandro
b. 1974

Maria Carolina
(b. 2003)

Maria Chiara
(b. 2005)

Antonio
(b. 2003)

Dorothée
(b. 2005)

Anna Sophia
b. 1999

Maria Isabel
b. 2012

Luisa Fernanda
b. 2014

Paulo Alfonso
b. 2014

EUROHISTORY.COM

A Two Sicilies Family Photo Album

In a family as prolific as the Bourbons of the Two Sicilies, infant mortality was a common happening. This is an allegorical painting picturing the early death of a Sicilian prince.

Princess Maria Amalia (1818-1857), daughter of King Francesco I, married her cousin Infante Sebastián of Spain.

Princess Antonia (1814-1898), daughter of King Francesco I, married her cousin Grand Duke Leopoldo II of Tuscany.

King Ferdinando I of the Two Sicilies. (1751-1825)

Infante Antonio (1755-1817), brother of King Ferdinando I. He married his niece Infanta Maria Amalia of Spain (1779-1798).

Infante Francisco Javier (1757-1771), the youngest brother of King Ferdinando I. Born at Caserta, he died at Aranjuez, Spain.

Infante Filippo (1747-1777) and his brother, the future King Carlos IV (18148-1819). Both born at the Royal Palace of Portici.

Infante Gabriel (1752-1788) was also born at Portici when his father Carlos III was King of the Two Sicilies.

Infanta Maria Josepha Carmela (1744-1801), sister of King Ferdinando I. She was born at Gaeta and died in Madrid.

Infanta Maria Luisa (1745-1792), wife of Holy Roman Emperor Leopold II. Born at Portici, she died in Vienna.

Infante Filippo (1747-1777), eldest son of King Carlos III, was Duke of Calabria. He was handicapped and passed over.

Queen Maria Amalia (née Saxony) was the wife of King Carlos III, who was first King of Naples and then King of Spain.

Queen Maria Carolina, consort of King Ferdinando I.

King Ferdinando I of the Two Sicilies.

Princess Maria Cristina (1779-1849), a daughter of Ferdinando I, was married to King Carlo Felice of Sardinia.

Archduchess Clementine of Austria (1777-1801), first wife of King Francesco I of the Two Sicilies.

Princess Maria Antonietta (1814-1898) was one of the daughters of King Francesco I and Queen Maria Isabel. Born in Palermo, during the dynasty's exile, she married her cousin Grand Duke Leopoldo II of Tuscany. Many of her descendants married into her Sicilian family.

Princess Maria Carolina (1820-1861), daughter of Francesco I, married in Caserta her cousin Infante Carlos of Spain, Count of Montemolín.

Empress Teresa Cristina of Brazil. (1822-1889)

From the left: Prince Antonio, the Count d'Eu, Prince Luiz, Prince Pedro de Alcântara, Princess Imperial Isabel, Emperor Pedro II, Empress Teresa Cristina and Prince Pedro Augusto of Saxe-Coburg & Gotha.

Princess Maria Carolina (11822-1869), daughter of the Prince and Princess of Salerno. Born in Vienna, she married in Naples the immensely wealthy Prince Henri d'Orléans, Duke d'Aumâle. Their main residence was the Château de Chantilly, in the vicinity of Paris.

Grand Duchess Maria Antonietta of Tuscany and daughter Archduchess Maria Luisa (1845-1917), who married Fürst Karl of Isenburg-Büdingen.

Archduchess Maria Annunziata of Austria and her children, Archdukes Franz Ferdinand and Otto c. 1865.

On June 28, 1914, shots were fired in Sarajevo that were heard around the world. The two victims of the heinous assassination were Archduke Franz Ferdinand of Austria and his wife the Duchess of Hohenberg. Since he was the heir of the Austro-Hungarian moanrchy, Vienna reacted to his death with shock and uproar. Within weeks Europe was at war and the world had changed forever. However, very few even knew that Archduke Franz Ferdinand was the grandson of King Ferdinando II.

After the assassination of his uncle Franz Ferdinand, Archduke Karl became the heir of his great-uncle Emperor Franz Joseph. Karl was not only the grandson of the former Princess Maria Annunziata of Bourbon-Two Sicilies, but he was married to Princess Zita, daughter of Duke Roberto of Parma from his second marriage. Roberto's first wife, Maria Pia, was one of the sisters of Karl of Austria's paternal mother, Maria Annunziata of the Two Sicilies.

Archduke Franz Salvator (1866-1939), son of the former Princess Maria Immaculata of Bourbon-Two Sicilies, married Archduchess Marie Valerie, youngest daughter of Emperor Franz Josef.

Archduchess Carolina (1869-1945) and her sister Archduchess Marie Antoinette (1874-1891). Carolina married Prince August Leopold of Saxe-Coburg & Gotha, a grandson of Empress Teresa Cristina of Brazil.

King Francesco II of the Two Sicilies.

Queen Maria Sophia of the Two Sicilies.

The last years of King Francesco II were clouded by his continued worsening health. The exiled King of the Two Sicilies visited the Tyrol frequently as his medical team considered the climate would do him much good. He was staying at Arco, in the South Tyrol, when he died on December 27, 1894. This is an image of his body laying in repose. It was customary then to take such images.

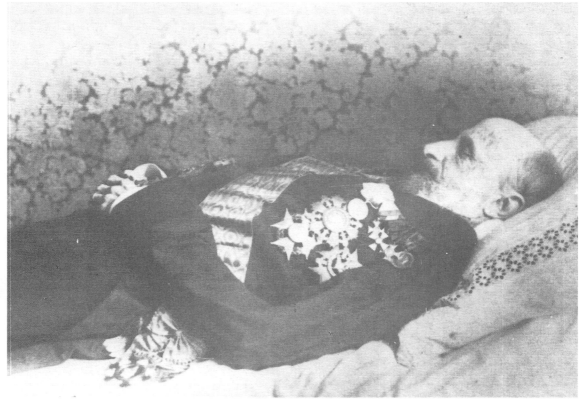

The Count of Caserta in the late 1850s.

The Countess of Caserta in the late 1850s.

The Countess of Caserta in 1895.

The Count of Caserta in old age.

The Duchess of Calabria and her daughter Princess Lucie visiting the Vatican, where Pope Pius XI received them.

Queen Mother Maria Cristina and her eldest grandson, the Infante Alfonso. During the reign of his uncle King Alfonso XIII, the Infante served in the Spanish military.

Infante Alfonso of Spain.
(1901-1964)

197

At the Vatican. From left: The Duke of Noto, the Infante don Carlos (Duke of Calabria), His Holiness Pope Benedict XVI, the Duchess of Calabria, the Duchess of Noto and the Duke of Capua.

The Duchess of Calabria with her mother the Countess of Paris.

The Dukes of Calabria with Queen Fabiola of Belgium.

Princess Cristina, Mrs. López-Quesada

Archduchess Maria of Austria.

Princess Inés, Nobile Michele Carelli Palombi.

Princess Victoria, Mrs. Markos Nomikos.

The Duke and Duchess of Noto.

The Duke of Capua.

Reconciliation: Naples, January 24, 2014. From left: The Duke of Noto, the Duchess of Castro, the Duchess of Calabria and the Duke of Castro.

TRH The Count and Countess of Barcelona.

The Duke and Duchess of Castro (Ferdinando and Chantal) and their son Prince Carlo, Duke of Calabria.

Prince Carlo of Bourbon-Two Sicilies, then Duke of Calabria.

The Duke of Castro escorting Camilla Crociani on her wedding day.

The Duke and Duchess of Castro with the Duke and Duchess of Bragança and their eldest son, the Prince of Beira – Portugal, 2014.

The Duke and Duchess of Castro.

The Duke of Noto and the Duke of Castro.

BIBLIOGRAPHY & SOURCES

Books

Acton, Harold. *The Bourbons of Naples (1734-1825)*. London: Methuen and Co Ltd, 1956.

___ *The Last Bourbons of Naples (1825-1861)*. London: Methuen and Co Ltd, 1961.

dell'Aja, P. Gaudenzio. *Il Pantheon dei Borboni in Santa Chiara di Napoli*. Napoli: Giannini, 1987.

Alexandre dos Santos, Armando. *Dom Pedro Henrique: O Condestável das Saudades e da Esperança*. São Paulo: Artpress, 2006.

Beéche, Arturo E. *Dear Ellen… Royal Europe Through the Photo Albums of H.I.H. Grand Duchess Helen Vladimirovna of Russia*. East Richmond Heights, CA: Eurohistory & Kensington House Books, 2011.

Bern, Stéphane. *Diane de France—La princesse rebelle*. Mayenne: Éditions Flammarion, 2003.

Boucher, Jean-Jacques. Charles Ferdinand d'Artois, duc de Berry (1778-1820). Paris: Éditions Fernand Lanore, 2000.

Bourcet, Marguerite. *Un couple de tragédie: le destin brisé du duc et de la duchesse d'Alençon*. Mesnil-sur-l'Estrée: Éditions Perrin, 2003.

Cannuyer, Christian. *Les Maisons Royales et Souveraines d'Europe*. Turnhout, Belgique: Editions Brepols, 1989.

Castronuovo, Sandro. *I Cinque Borbone: La Dinastia Napoletana dal 1734 al 1860*. Napoli: Altrastampa Edizioni, 2000.

Enache, Nicolas. *La Descendance de Marie-Thérèse de Habsburg, Reine de Hongrie et de Bohême*. Paris: L'Intermédiaire des Chercheurs et Curieux, 1996.

Felice, Gaetano de. *Il Re: Alfonso di Borbone Conte di Caserta*. Nocera Sup.: D'Amico Editore, 2013.

Gentile, Aniello. *Da Gaeta ad Arco: Diario di Francesco II di Borbone (1 gennaio 1862 – 24 dicembre 1894)*. Napoli: Arte Tipografica, 1988.

González de Vega, Javier. *Yo, María de Borbón: la autobiografía dictada por la Madre del Rey*. 4th ed. Madrid: Ediciones El País, 2000.

Gracia, Fernando. *La madre del Rey—La vida de doña María de las Mercedes: una causa histórica*. Madrid: Ediciones Temas de Hoy, 1994.

Grèce, Michel de. *Mémoires insolites*. Paris: XO Éditions, 2004.

Guillon, Amiral Jacques. *François d'Orléans, Prince de Joinville*. Paris, Éditions France-Empire, 1990.

Hamann, Brigitte. *Die Habsburger: Ein biographisches Lexikon*. München: R. Piper GmbH & Co. KG, 1988.

Hibbert, Christopher. *Garibaldi and his enemies: The clash of arms and personalities in the making of Italy*. Boston: Little, Born and Copmpany, 1966.

Huberty, Michel, et al. *L'Allemagne Dynastique—Tome I: Hesse-Reuss-Saxe*. Le Perreux: Privately printed, 1976.

Lorenz, Sönke, et al. *Das Haus Württemberg: Ein biographisches Lexikon*. Stuttgart: W. Kolhammer GmbH, 1997.

Marini Dettina, Alfonso. *Il Legittimo Esercizio del Gran Magistero del Sacro Militare Ordine Costantiniano di San Giorgi*. Roma: Libreria Editrice Vaticana, 2003.

Márquez de la Plata, Vicenta María and Luis Valero de Bernabé. *El libro de oro de los duques*. Madrid: Prensa y Ediciones Iberoamericanas.

Mateos Sáinz de Medrano, Ricardo. *Eulalia de Borbón: l'enfant terrible*. Pozuelo de Alarcón: Alberdi Ediciones, 2014.

___ *Los Borbones: imagenes para la historia de una familia real*. Madrid: La Esfera de los Libros, 2007.

___ *Los desconocidos infantes de España*. Barcelona: Editorial Thassàlia, 1996.

___ *Los infantes de Andalucía*. Madrid: Velecío Editores, 2005.

___ *La Reina María Cristina: Madre de Alfonso XIII y regente de España*. Madrid: La Esfera de los Libros, 2007.

McIntosh, David. *The Unknown Habsburgs—Tuscany*. Falköping, Sweden: Rosvall Royal Books, 2000.

Miller, Ilana D. and Arturo E. Beéche. *Royal Gatherings: Who is in the Picture… Volume I: 1859-1914*. East Richmond Heights, CA: Eurohistory & Kensington House Books, 2012.

___ *Royal Gatherings: Who is in the Picture… Volume II: 1914-1939*. East Richmond Heights, CA: Eurohistory & Kensington House Books, 2015.

Minet, Paul. *Royalty Digest: a Journal of Record: Volume 3*. Ticehurst, East Sussex: Royalty Digest, 1994.

___ *Royalty Digest: a Journal of Record: Volume 10*. Ticehurst, East Sussex: Royalty Digest, 2001.

___ *Royalty Digest: a Journal of Record: Volume 12*. Ticehurst, East Sussex: Royalty Digest, 2003.

___ *Royalty Digest: a Journal of Record: Volume 14*. Ticehurst, East Sussex: Royalty Digest, 2005.

Montjouvent, Philippe de. *Le Comte de Paris et sa descendance*. Paris: Éditions du Chaney, 1998.

Nicolay, Comtesse René de. *Le temps de ma mère : souvenirs*. Privately printed.

Paoli, Dominique. *La Duchesse d'Alençon—Sophie-Charlotte, sœur de Sissi*. Bruxelles: Éditions Racines, 1999.

Paris, Isbaelle, Comtesse de. *Tout m'est bonheur*. Paris: Robert Laffont – Opera mundi, 1978.

___*Tout m'est bonheur: Les chemins creux*. Paris: Robert Laffont – Opera mundi, 1981.

Praschl-Bichler, Gabriele. *Das Familienalbum von Kaiser Karl und Kaiserin Zita*. Wien: Ueberreuter, 1996.

Puga, María Teresa and Eusebio Ferrer. *20 Infantas de España*. Barcelona: Editorial Juventud, 1998.

Rayón, Fernando. *La Boda de Juan Carlos y Sofía: claves y secretos de un enlace histórico*. Madrid: La Esfera de los Libros, 2002.

Rubio, María José. *La Chata: La Infanta Isabel de Borbón y la corona de España*. Madrid: La Esfera de los Libros, 2003.

de Sagrera, Ana. *Ena y Bee: En defensa de una amistad*. Madrid: Velecío Editores, 2005.

de Sangro, Michele. *I Borboni nel Regno delle Due Sicilie*. Lecce: Capone Editore, 2004.

Stair Sainty, Guy. *The Orders of Chivalry and Merit of the Bourbon Two Sicilies Dynasty*. Madrid: S.M.O.C.S.G., 1989.

de Stoeckl, Agnes. *King of the French: A Portrait of Louis Philippe 1773-1850*. London: John Murray, 1957.

Tourtchine, Jean-Fred. *Les Manuscrits du CEDRE: Le Royaume d'Italie Volume III*. Paris: C.E.D.R.E., 1994.

___ *Les Manuscrits du CEDRE: Le Royaume des Deux Sicilies Volume II et Le Royaume de Grèce*. Paris: C.E.D.R.E., 1998.

Van Kerrebrouck, Patrick. *La Maison de Bourbon 1256-2004: Tome IV*. 2nd ed. Villeneuve d'Ascq: Privately published, 2004.

Wrangel, Comte F.U. *Les Maisons Souveraines de l'Europe: Volume I*. Stockholm: Collektion Hasse W-Tullberg, 1907.

___ *Les Maisons Souveraines de l'Europe: Volume II*. Stockholm: Collektion Hasse W-Tullberg, 1899.

Newspapers & Periodicals

ABC

Chicago Tribune

El Confidencial

EUROHISTORY: The European Royal History Journal

Harper's Bazaar

Harper's New Monthly Magazine

Hola!

Illustrated London News

L'Illustration

Point de Vue

The New York Times

The Telegraph

The Times of London

The Washington Post

INDEX

A

Acton, Harold 16, 19
D'Annunzio, Gabriele 47
Apovian, Christine (formerly de Bourbon) 183
Arco-Zinneberg, Sophie-Leopoldine, Countess von 67
Auffenberg, General 115

Austria

Albrecht, Archduke of, Duke of Teschen 56
Elisabeth, Empress of (née Bavaria) 27, 29, 31, 39, 45-46
Elisabeth, Archduchess of 71
Ferdinand Karl, Archduke of 32
Franz II, Emperor of 7
Franz Ferdinand, Archduke of 27, 31-32
Franz Joseph, Emperor of 30-31, 43, 51, 56, 115, 119
Franz Karl, Archduke of 31
Friedrich, Archduke of, Duke of Teschen 83, 94
Josef, Archduke of 88
Karl I, Emperor of 27, 102, 115, 117, 181
Karl Ferdinand, Archduke of 56
Karl Ludwig, Archduke of 27, 31, 37
Karl Stefan, Archduke of 30
Katharina, Archduchess of (née Isenburg) 181-182
Leopold II, Emperor of 10
Margherita, Archduchess of (née Savoy-Aosta) 181-182
Maria, Archduchess of (née Two Sicilies) 101-102
Maria Annunziata, Archduchess of (née Two Sicilies) 27, 31-32, 37, 119
Maria Josepha, Archduchess of 5-6
Maria Theresa, Empress of 5
Maria Theresa, Empress of (née Two Sicilies) 7
Maria Theresa, Archduchess of (née Tuscany) 30
Martin, Archduke of 181
Otto, Archduke of 31
Robert, Archduke of 181
Rudolf, Crown Prince of 31, 71
Simeon, Archduke of 102
Sophie, Archduchess of (née Bavaria) 31
Zita, Empress of (née Parma) 102, 115, 117, 181

B

Balzo, Count Francisco del 16, 18
Baumbach, Andreas 174-175

Bavaria

Amelia, Princess of (née Spain) 67
Franz, Prince of 119, 129
Isabella, Princess of (née Croÿ) 119, 129
Ludovika, Duchess in (née Bavaria) 39
Ludwig II, King of 61
Ludwig III, King of 9, 61-62
Luitpold, Prince Regent of 61-62
Max, Duke in 39
Otto, King of 61-62

Belgium

Albert I, King of 159
Albert II, King of 181
Astrid, Princess of, Archduchess of Austria 181
Laurent, Prince of 153, 155
Leopold II, King of 9, 71, 147, 159
Lorenz, Archduke of Austria, Prince of 181
Marie Henriette, Queen of 147
Philippe, Count of Flanders 159

Bentinck, Lord William 13
Bernstorff, Countess 25

Bonaparte

Alix, Princess Napoléon (née de Foresta) 146
Princess Caroline Napoléon, Mme Eric Quérénet-Onfroy de Bréville 147
Prince Charles Napoléon 146-147
Clementine, Princess Napoléon (née Belgium) 71, 147
Jean-Christophe, Prince Napoléon 147
Joseph, King of Spain 7
Louis, Prince Napoléon 146
Marie Louise, Empress of the French (née Austria) 7-8
Napoleon I, Emperor of the French 7-8, 13
Napoleon II, King of Rome 7, 9
Napoleon III, Emperor of the French 51
Victor, Prince Napoléon 146

Borbón y Vallabriga, María Luisa de 103

Brazil (Orléans-Bragança)

Afonso, Prince of 92
Antonio, Prince of 122, 125
Cristina, Princess of 92
Elizabeth, Princess of (née Dobrzensky von Dobrzenicz) 83, 92, 122
Esperanza, Princess of (née Two Sicilies) 78, 84, 91-93, 97
Francisco, Prince of 92
Gaston, Count d'Eu (né France) 9, 82, 92, 122, 126, 159, 168
Isabelle, Princess of 130
Isabel, Princess Imperial of 9, 82, 92, 122, 125
Luiz, Prince of 56, 58, 122, 125
Luiz Gastão, Prince of 122, 127, 129
Luiz Gastão, Prince Imperial of 129
Manoel, Prince of 92
Maria, Princess of (née Bavaria) 119, 129-130
Maria da Glória, Princess of, Duchess of Segorbe (formerly Yugoslavia) 92-93
Maria Pia, Princess of (née Two Sicilies) 53, 58, 119, 122, 126-127, 129-131, 137, 159
Pedro II, Emperor of 9, 13, 21, 31, 122
Pedro de Alcântara, Prince of Grão Pará 82-83, 122, 126
Pedro de Alcântara, Prince of 92
Pedro Gastão, Prince of 84, 92-93, 122, 129
Pedro Henrique, Prince of 119, 122, 125, 129-131, 173
Pia Maria, Princess of 125, 131
Teresa, Princess of 83, 92
Teresa Cristina, Empress of (née Two Sicilies) 13, 21, 31, 122

Bulgaria
Ferdinand, King of 9, 34
Giovanna, Queen Mother of 88
Maria Luisa, Princess of (née Parma) 34
Marie Louise, Princess of 88
Simeon II, King of 88, 98

C

Carelli Palombi, Nobile Michele 102
Causans, Count Rodolphe de 183
Chaponay, Antoine, Marquis de 149
Chaponay, Geneviève, Marquise de (née Orléans) 149
Chias Osorio, Carlos 92
Cochin, Denis, Baron 149
Cochin, Dorothée 149
Cochin, Jacques 149
Cochin, Nicolas 149
Cochin, Thérèse, Baroness (née de Fréval de Ribains) 149
Creutz, Count Carl Fredrik 175
Crociani, Camillo 151
Crociani, Edoarda (née Vesselovsky) 151

Czartoryski
Prince Adam, Duke of Klewan and Zukow 83, 90, 168
Prince Adam Karol 91
Princess Dolores (née Two Sicilies) 78, 83-84, 90-92, 97
Prince Josef-August 83, 90-92
Prince Ludwik 91
Princess Maria-Ludovika (née Krasinska) 90
Princess Marguerite (née Orléans) 83, 90, 168

D

Delcarretto, Marquis 14

Denmark
Frederik VIII, King of 132
Frederik, Crown Prince of 155
Louise, Queen of 132

F

France
Charles X, King of 10
Charles, Duke de Berry 10
Charles Philippe, Duke de Nemours
Emanuel, Duke of Vendôme 159, 162, 164, 168
Ferdinand, Duke d'Alençon 159, 168
Ferdinand, Duke de Montpensier 134
Henri, Count de Chambord 9-10, 51, 52
Henri, Count of Paris 75, 82, 88, 92, 97-99, 101, 140, 179, 183
Henri, Count of Paris (b.1933) 120
Henriette, Duchess of Vendôme (née Belgium) 159, 164
Isabelle, Countess of Paris (née Spain) 78-80
Isabelle, Duchess de Guise (née Orléans) 179
Isabelle, Countess of Paris (née Orléans-Bragança) 82, 88, 92, 130
Jean, Duke de Guise 79, 179, 183
Jean, Duke de Vendôme 120
Louis, Duke de Nemours 90, 168
Louis Philippe, King of the French 7, 10, 19, 147
Marguerite, Duchess de Nemours (née Watson) 159

Marie, Princess d'Orleans 19
Marie-Amélie, Queen of the French (née Two Sicilies) 7, 10, 19, 90, 147, 174
Marie Antoinette, Queen of (née Austria) 5
Marie Caroline, Duchess de Berry (née Two Sicilies) 10, 13, 20, 34
Marie Isabelle, Countess of Paris (née Spain) 9
Marie-Louise, Princess of (formerly Two Sicilies, then Mrs. Kingsland) 59, 159-160, 164
Marie-Thérèse, Duchess of Montpensier (née Württemberg) 120
Philippe, Count of Paris 9, 78
Philippe, Duke d'Orléans 78
Robert, Duke of Chartres 9
Sophie, Duchesse d'Alençon 46, 159
Sophie, Princess of 159
Victoire, Duchess de Nemours (née Saxe-Coburg & Gotha) 168

Francis (Pope) 108
Franco, Francisco 84, 89, 95
Frioli, Alberto 68

G

Ganem Rubião, Maria da Glória 183
García de Saéz, Miguel 170
Garibaldi, Giuseppe 20, 27, 28, 40-41, 49, 51

Germany
Wilhelm II, German Kaiser 66

Gladstone, William (British prime minister) 25
Gómez-Acebo y de Estrada, don Luis, Duke of Badajoz 89
Gonzaga Maldonado y Gordon, Luis 170

Greece
Christopher, Prince of 179
Françoise, Princess of (née France) 179
Frederica, Queen of the Hellenes (née Hannover) 97
Michael, Prince of 179
Paul, King of the Hellenes 97

H

Hohenzollern
Leopold, Fürst von 45
Maria Teresa, Fürstin von (née Two Sicilies) 29-30, 53, 57
Wilhelm, Fürst von 30

I

Italy
Umberto I, King of 47
Umberto II, King of 65, 88
Vittorio Emanuele II, formerly King of Sardinia, King of 9, 40
Vittorio Emanuele III, King of 88

K

Kingsland, Walter 160, 164
Koenig, Marlene Eilers 104

L

Laula, don Íñigo Moreno y Arteaga, 12th Marquis de 98
Lazinsky, Tomasz 138

Liechtenstein
Georg, Prince of 120
Marie Christine, Princess of (née Württemberg) 120

López-Quesada, Pedro 102

Lubomirski
Prince Kasimir 168
Princess Therese (née Granow-Wodzicka) 168

Luchesi Palli
Countess Beatrice (née Parma) 34
Count Pietro 34

M

Martorell, Ernesto 83
Mateos Sainz de Medrano, Ricardo 177

Mecklenburg-Schwerin
Anastasia Mikhailovna, Grand Duchess of (née Russia) 53

Medinaceli
de Medina y Fernández de Córdoba, don Ignacio, Duke of Segorbe 93
de Medina y Orléans-Bragança, Luna 93
de Medina y Orléans-Bragança, Sol 93
Medinaceli, Duchess of 93

Melgarejo y Saurín, don Joaquín de 103

Mexico
Carlota, Empress of (née Belgium) 9

Migliaccio, Donna Lucia 8

Modena (Este)
Ferdinando, Duke of 67
Maria Leopoldine, Archduchess of 67

Monaco
Rainier III, Prince of 153
Albert II, Prince 153, 155

Morales y Aguado, don Luis de 98

Murat
Joachim, King of Naples 7, 8

N

Nelson, Admiral Horatio 7
Nicolay, Count René de 131
Nomikos, Markos 102
Nomikos, P. 102

O

Orléans-Borbón
Alvaro, Prince of 92
Ataúlfo, Prince of 92
Carla, Princess of 92

P

Parma
Augusto, Prince of (b. and d. 1882) 34
Carlo III, Duke of 21, 34
Elias, Duke of 34, 83, 94, 102
Enrico, Count of Bardi 27, 34, 38, 52
Enrico, Prince of 34
Ferdinando, Prince of 34
Guiseppe, Prince of 34
Louise, Duchess of (née France) 9-10, 20, 21, 34
Maria Anna, Duchess of (née Austria) 34, 83, 94
Maria Antonia, Duchess of (née Bragança) 102
Maria Luisa, Countess of Bardi (née Two Sicilies) 27, 34, 35, 38
Maria Pia, Duchess of (née Two Sicilies) 9, 27, 34, 38, 83, 94, 102, 115
Roberto I, Duke of 9, 27, 34, 38, 45, 52, 102, 115

Pius IX (Pope) 25, 29, 41, 51

Portugal
Amelie, Queen of (née Orléans) 78
Duarte Nuño, Duke of Bragança 88
Francisca, Duchess of Bragança (née Orléans-Bragança) 88
Maria II, Queen of 9, 110

Powell, Maureen Marjorie (formerly de Bourbon) 166
Presenzano, Duke of 16

Prussia
Georg Friedrich, Prince of 182
Sophie, Princess of (née Isenburg) 182

Q

Quérénet-Onfroy de Bréville
Augustin 147
Elvire 147
Eric 147

R

Romania
Carol II, King of 88
Ferdinand, King of 30

Russia
Alexander II, Tsar of 51
Maria Pavlovna, Grand Duchess of (née Mecklenburg-Schwerin) 78
Olga Alexandrovna, Grand Duchess of 132
Vladimir Alexandrovich, Grand Duke of 78

S

San Fernando de Quiroga, Duke of 103

Sardinia
Carlo-Felice, King of 7
Cristina, Queen of (née Two Sicilies) 7
Vittorio Emanuele I, King of 25

Savoy
Amedeo, 1st Duke of Aosta, King of Spain 52
Amedeo, 3rd Duke of Aosta 179, 181-182
Anne, Duchess of Aosta (née France) 179, 183
Elisabeth, Duchess of Genoa (née Bavaria) 67
Eugenio, first Duke of Ancona, then Duke of Genoa 64-65, 67
Guiseppe, Count of Villafranca 19
Isabella, Princess of Savoy-Genoa 67-68
Lucia, first Duchess of Ancona, then Duchess of Genoa (née Two Sicilies) 62, 64-65, 67
Maria, Princess of 88
Tommaso, Duke of Genoa 67

Saxe-Coburg & Gotha
August Leopold, Prince of 31
Carolina, Princess of (née Tuscany) 31

Saxony
Alexander, Prince of, Margrave of Meißen 119
Friedrich August III, King of 113
Georg, Crown Prince of 110
Gisela, Princess of, Margravine of Meißen (née Bavaria) 119
Johann Georg, Prince of 58, 65, 110, 113
Maria Ana, Crown Princess of (née Portugal) 110
Maria Immacolata, Princess of (née Two Sicilies) 53, 57-58, 110, 113, 132, 140
Maria Isabella, Princess of (née Württemberg) 110

Schmuckher, Baron von 16

Schönborn-Wiesentheid
Franz Clemens, Count von 174
Tatjana, Countess von (née Gortschakow) 174

Schuschnigg, Chancellor 117
Sotomayor y Luna, dom Manuel 64

Spain
Alfonso XII, King of 32-33, 52
Alfonso XIII, King of 34, 54, 57, 71, 76-82, 86-87, 93, 98, 104, 134, 136, 138, 140, 168, 173
Alfonso, Prince of Asturias 76, 87
Alfonso, Infante of 88-89
Antoine, Duke of Montpensier, Infante of Spain (né France) 78, 80, 84
Antonia, Queen of (née Two Sicilies) 7
Antonio, Duke of Galliera 9
Carlos III, King of 74, 103
Carlos IV, King of 7, 13
Carlos, Infante of (1818-1861) 13
Carlos, Duke of Madrid 31, 52
Elena, Infanta of, Duchess of Lugo 104
Felipe V, King of 103
Felipe VI, King of 85, 104
Ferdinando VI, King of 5
Ferdinando VII, King of 7, 13, 103
Fernando, Prince of Bavaria, Infante of 79, 92
Francisco de Asis, King Consort of 9, 13

Francisco de Paula, Infante of 13
Gonzalo, Infante of 87
Isabel II, Queen of 9, 13, 21-22, 27, 32, 51-53, 78, 80
Jaime, Infante of Spain 87
Juan, Count of Barcelona 75, 83, 87-90, 95, 97
Juan Carlos I, King of 75, 83, 85, 88-90, 92, 95-98, 102, 134, 173, 177
Luis, Infante of, former Archbishop of Toledo 103
Luis Alfonso, Prince of Bavaria, Infante of 92
Luisa Carlotta, Infanta of (née Two Sicilies) 13, 67
Luisa Fernanda, Infanta of Spain, Duchess of Montpensier 78, 80
Margarita, Infanta of, Duchess of Soria 88-89, 104
Margherita, Duchess of Madrid (née Parma) 52
María, Countess of Barcelona (née Two Sicilies) 78-79, 83, 86-90, 134, 177
Maria Amelia, Infanta of (née Two Sicilies) 13
Maria Carolina, Infanta of (née Two Sicilies) 13
Maria Cristina, Queen of (née Two Sicilies) 13
Maria Cristina, Queen Regent of (née Austria) 54-56, 61-62, 71, 78, 83, 85, 134
María Cristina, Infanta of 104
María de las Mercedes, Princess of Asturias 32, 53, 58, 65, 71, 74, 76-77, 80, 93
Maria Luisa, Queen of (née Parma) 13
María del Pilar, Infanta of, Duchess of Badajoz 88-89
María Teresa, Infanta of 71, 79, 92
Mercedes, Queen of 9
Sebastian, Infante of 13
Sofía, Queen of 89, 96-97, 177, 179
Victoria Eugenia, Queen of (née Battenberg) 78, 87

Stolberg-Wernigerode
Anton, Count zu 67
Barbara, Countess zu (née Two Sicilies) 62, 64, 67-68
Elisabeth, Countess zu (née Waldburg zu Wolfegg u. Waldsee) 67
Elizabeth, Countess zu 67
Franz-Xavier, Count zu 64, 67
Sophie, Countess zu 67

T
Tanucci, Bernardo 5

Tuscany
Albrecht Salvator, Archduke of 30
Alicia, Grand Duchess of (née Parma) 115
Blanca, Archduchess of (née Spain)
Dorothea, Archduchess of (née Bavaria) 117, 129
Ferdinando III, Grand Duke of 7
Ferdinando IV, Grand Duke of 9, 115
Franz Salvator, Archduke of 31
Georg, Archduke of 115, 119
Gottfried, Archduke of 115, 117, 129
Joseph Ferdinand, Archduke of 117
Karl Salvator, Archduke of 27, 30-31, 37
Leopold Salvator, Archduke of 31
Leopoldo, Grand Duke of 13
Luisa, Grand Duchess of (née Two Sicilies) 7
Luisa, Archduchess of (formerly Saxony) 113
Maria Antonietta, Grand Duchess of (née Two Sicilies) 13, 30
Maria Christina, Archduchess of (née Two Sicilies) 53, 58, 115, 117, 119, 174
Maria Immacolata, Archduchess of (née Two Sicilies) 27, 30-31, 37
Marie Valerie, Archduchess of (née Austria) 31

Marie Valerie, Archduchess of (née Waldburg-Zeil) 119
Peter Ferdinand, Archduke of 58, 66, 115, 117, 119
Sigismund, Archduke of 120

Two Sicilies
Adrian, Prince de Bourbon 164, 166
Alberto, Prince of (1792-1798) 7
Alberto, Count of Castrogiovanni 27, 37, 49
Alessandro, Prince of (priest) 183
Alexandra, Princess of (née Schönborn-Wiesentheid) 174
Alfonso, Count of Caserta 9, 23, 27, 34, 37, 49, 51-57, 66, 71, 79, 82-83, 96, 120, 129, 134, 136, 138, 162, 168, 174
Alfonso, Infante of Spain, Duke of Calabria 68, 72, 74-76, 83, 90, 92-98, 140-141, 144
Alfonso, Prince of 120
Alicia, Infanta of Spain, Duchess of Calabria (née Parma) 34, 83, 92, 94-95, 98, 102
Amelia Bellow-Hamel, Countess of Roccaguglielma 22
Anna, Princess of (1775-1780) 7
Anna Sofia, Princess of 183
Anna Cecilia, Princess of 183
Anne, Duchess of Calabria (née France) 96, 98-99, 101-102, 120
Anne, Princess of (formerly Cochin) 146, 149
Antonietta, Countess of Caserta (née Two Sicilies) 9, 23, 34, 51, 56-57, 66, 79, 83, 86, 113, 129, 134, 136, 138, 168, 174
Antonio, Count of Lecce 13, 18, 20-21, 34
Antonio, Prince of 120, 141, 168, 170, 174
Beatrice Bordessa, Countess di Villa Colli 59, 130, 134, 136-137
Beatrice, Princess of (formerly Napoléon) 146-147
Blanca, Princess of 104
Blanche Marconnay, wife of Prince Pasquale 35, 38
Camilla, Duchess of Castro (née Crociani) 108, 151, 153, 155
Carlo, Prince of (1775-1778) 7
Carlo, Prince of (1788-1789) 7
Carlo, Duke of Castro 69, 76, 104, 108, 144-146, 149, 151, 153, 155
Carlo Ferdinando, Prince of Capua 13-14, 18, 40
Carlo(s), Infante of Spain, Prince of 32, 51, 53-54, 58, 61, 65, 68, 71-72, 74, 76-87, 89-93
Carlos, Infante of Spain, Prince of 78, 83, 90
Carlos, Infante of Spain, Duke of Calabria 34, 68, 75-76, 94-99, 101-104, 108-109, 144
Carrie-Ann, Princess de Bourbon (née Thornley) 166
Carolina, Duchess of Castro (née Zamoyska) 59, 83, 138, 140, 144
Casimiro, Prince of 141, 173, 179, 181, 183
Cecilia, Princess of (née Lubomirska) 59, 168, 170, 173, 179
Chantal, Princess of (née de Chevron-Villette) 144, 146
Christian Peter de Bourbon 166
Clementine, Princess of (née Austria) 7
Clotilde, Princess of (1786-1792) 7
Cristina, Princess of 101-102
Elena Sofia, Princess of 183
Elisabeth, Princess of (née Württemberg) 120, 174
Enricheta, Princess of (1787-1792) 7
Ferdinando I, King of 5-10, 13, 74, 78, 90, 103, 147, 174
Ferdinando II, King of 13-14, 16, 19-20, 23-25, 27, 29-30, 34, 37, 39, 49, 94
Ferdinando, Duke of Castro 75-76, 98, 138, 141, 144-146, 149, 153
Ferdinando-Pio, Duke of Calabria 54, 58, 61-62, 65-68, 74, 96, 131, 140, 144, 168
Fernando, Infante of Spain, Prince of 76-77
Filippo, Prince of (1847-1922) 22
Filippo, Prince of (1885-1949) 53, 59, 159-160, 162, 168
Francesco I, King of 7, 10, 13-14, 18-19, 24, 67, 92, 103

Francesco II, King of 9, 14, 20, 22-23, 25, 27-29, 33, 39-41, 43-47, 49, 54-55, 104
Francesco, Prince of (b.1960) 174
Francesco d'Assisi, Prince of (1888-1914) 53, 56, 59, 136
Francesco di Paolo, Count of Trapani 13, 18, 22-23, 51
Francesco di Paolo, Prince of (1873-1876) 53, 58, 136
Gabriele, Prince of 53, 59, 90, 120, 141, 168, 170, 173, 179
Gaetano, Count of Girgenti 27, 32-33, 37, 53
Gaetano, Prince of 162, 164
Gennaro, Prince of (1780-1789) 7
Gennaro, Count of Caltagirone 27, 29, 38
Gennaro, Prince of, Count di Villa Colli (1882-1944) 53, 59, 130, 134, 136-137
Gennaro, Prince of (b.1966) 175
Giovanni, Prince of 141, 170, 175, 177
Giuseppe, Prince of (1781-1783) 7
Giuseppe, Count of Lucera 27, 38
Gregory, Prince de Bourbon 164, 166
Inés, Princess of 94, 98
Inés, Princess of 102
Isabel, Countess of Girgenti (née Spain) 27, 32-34, 38, 53
Isabel Alfonsa, Infanta of Spain, Princess of, Countess Zamoyski 77, 81-82, 85-86
Isabella, Princess of (1793-1801) 7
Isabella, Countess of Trapani (née Tuscany) 13, 23, 51
Januaria, Countess of Aquila (née Brazil) 13, 21-22
Jaime, Duke of Capua 104, 108, 109
Juan, Prince of 104
Leopold, Prince of 7
Leopoldo, Count of Siricusa 13, 18-20, 22, 40
Linda Rose, Princess de Bourbon (née Idensohn) 166
Lodovico, Count of Trani 27, 29, 37, 39-40, 51, 53-54
Luigi, Count of Aquila 13, 18, 21-22
Luigi, Count of Roccaguglielma 21-22
Luisa, Infanta of Spain, Princess of (née Orléans) 58, 78-81, 83, 85, 91-92
Luisa Fernanda, Princess of 183
Luis Alfonso, Prince of 183
Malgorzata (Margarita), Princess of (née Czartoryska) 90, 120, 168
Maria, Princess of (1779-1783) 7
Maria, Princess of (b.2015) 104
Maria Annunziata, Princess of, Countess Creutz 175
Maria Antonietta, Princess of 62, 64
Maria del Carmen, Princess of 138, 144
Maria Carolina, Queen of (née Austria) 6-9, 67, 78, 90, 101, 147, 174
Maria Carolina, Princess of (b.1962) 174
Maria Carolina, Princess of, Duchess of Palermo 108, 153
Maria Chiara, Princess of, Duchess of Capri 108, 153
Maria Clementina, Queen of (née Austria) 10
Maria Cristina, Queen of (née Savoy) 25, 49, 76, 104
Maria Cristina, Princess (b. and d. 1870) 43, 47
Maria Cristina, Princess of 62, 64
Maria Cristina, Princess of (née Savoy-Aosta) 173, 179, 181-183
Maria Guiseppina, Princess of 53, 59, 130, 132, 137
Maria Immaculata, Princess of 170
Maria Isabel, Queen of (née Spain) 10, 14, 16, 18, 54
Maria Isabel, Princess of 183
Maria Margherita, Princess of 170
Maria Sophia, Queen of (née Bavaria) 28-29, 37, 39-41, 43, 45-47, 53, 55, 57, 159
Maria Theresa, Queen of (née Austria) 23, 25, 27-30, 34, 39, 43, 49, 56, 94
Maria Vittoria, Countess of Siricusa (née Savoy) 13, 19, 20

Marie, Duchess of Calabria (née Bavaria) 58, 61-62, 65-68
Mathilde, Countess of Trani (née Bavaria) 27, 29-30, 37, 39, 45, 53
Michelle Laura de Bourbon 166
Odette Labori, wife of Prince Filippo 59, 160, 162
Olivia de Bourbon (née Yarrow) 164
Pablo, Prince of 104
Paulo Alfonso, Prince of 183
Pasquale, Count of Bari 27, 35, 38
Pedro, Duke of Noto 69, 76, 102-104, 108-109, 144-145
Pedro, Prince of 104
Penelope Smyth, Countess of Mascali 13-14
Philippe Charles de Bourbon 166
Ranieri, Duke of Castro 53, 59, 68, 74-75, 83, 96-98, 138, 140-141, 144
Raymond de Bourbon 166
Ruggerio, Prince of 62, 64-65
Sofía, Duchess of Noto (née Landaluce y Melgarejo) 103-104, 108-109
Sofía, Princess of 104
Teresa, Princess of 94, 98
Urraca, Princess of 62, 65, 141
Victoria, Princess of 102
Vincenzo, Count of Milazzo 27, 38

U
United Kingdom
Alexandra, Queen of the 78, 132
Edward VII, King of the 78
Elizabeth II, Queen of the 179
Philip, Duke of Edinburgh 179
Victoria, Queen of the 9, 132, 168
Victoria, Princess of the 132

V
Vallabriga, María Teresa de 103

W
Wied
Carl, Fürst zu 182
Isabelle, Fürstin zu (née Isenburg) 182

Württemberg
Carl, Duke of 120, 177
Diane, Duchess of (née France) 120, 177
Friedrich, Duke of 120
Helene, Duchess of (née Tuscany) 115, 120
Margarete Sophie, Duchess of (née Austria) 32, 119
Maria Immacolata, Duchess of (née Tuscany) 31
Maria Theresa, Duchess of (née Austria) 110
Mathilde, Duchess of 177
Philipp, Duke of 9, 110
Philipp Albrecht, Duke of 119-120, 174
Robert, Duke of 31
Rosa, Duchess of (née Tuscany) 115, 120, 174

Y
Yarrow, Lt. Com. Charles 164

Yugoslavia
Alexander, Crown Prince of 93
Alexander, Prince of 93
Alexandra, Queen of (née Greece) 93
Peter II, King of 93
Peter, Prince of 93
Philip, Prince of 93

Z
Zamoyski
Andrzej, Count 23, 86
Jan-Kanty, Count 82, 86
Josef, Count 86
Karol, Count 86
Maria Carolina, Countess (née Two Sicilies) 23, 86, 138
Maria Cristina, Countess 86
Maria Teresa, Countess 86

Zurita, Dr. Carlos, Duke of Soria 89

The Coburgs of Europe

A royal biography of the Saxe-Coburg & Gotha dynasty and all its branches in Great Britain, Belgium, Portugal, Bulgaria and Coburg.

Queen Victoria and the Prince Consort were both Coburgs and they feature prominently in the storyline of each of the dynasty's branches.

It includes more than 500 photos of the various Coburg branches.

The price of this hardback book is: USA price: $48.95 + shipping ($8 in the USA – $26.00 overseas).

WE SHIP WORLDWIDE!

To order by phone: (510) 236-1730 or email: books@eurohistory.com

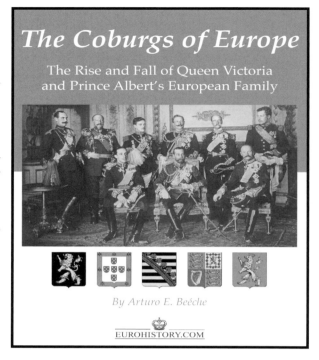

Russia and Europe – Dynastic Ties

Authored by Galina Korneva and Tatiana Cheboksarova, it includes nearly 600 photos, an overwhelming majority among them collected from the main archives of Russia and several European countries. The moment captured by these original photos is able, often times, to tell the reader far more about the unique world of royalty and aristocracy than countless pages of text. The authors also relied on important information obtained from Russian and foreign periodicals, memoirs and scientific literature. The English-language version of this book was expanded with contributions written by Arturo Beéche, founder and publisher of Eurohistory.

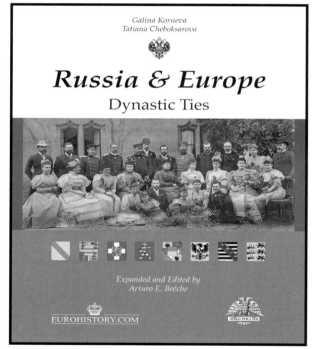

The price of this hardback book is: USA price: $49.95 + shipping ($8 in the USA – $26.00 overseas).

WE SHIP WORLDWIDE!

To order by phone: (510) 236-1730 or email: books@eurohistory.com

The Grand Dukes

Sons and Grandsons of Russia's Tsars

Included in this unique work, the First Volume in a two-volume series, are biographies of Russian grand dukes who were sons of Tsars or Claimants. These grand dukes came from the senior lines of the Russian Imperial Family at the time of the Revolution in 1917. The book is illustrated with exquisite and rare photographs of these intriguing men, their families and descendants. It also includes several family trees. The chapters were authored by some of today's most recognized authors and scholars on the Romanov Dynasty.

The price of this hardback book is: USA price: $43.95 plus $8 shipping and handling. International shipping and handling: $26.00 – WE SHIP WORLDWIDE! To order by phone: (510) 236-1730 or email: books@eurohistory.com

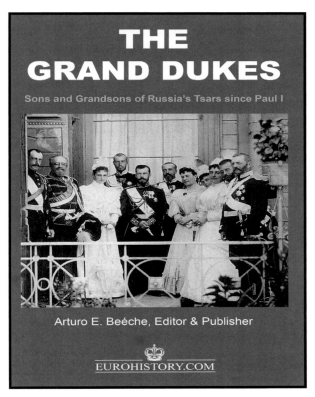

The Other Grand Dukes

Sons and Grandsons of Russia's Grand Dukes

Included in this unique work, the Second Volume in a two-volume series, are 18 biographies of Russian grand dukes. These grand dukes came from the junior lines of the Russian Imperial Family at the time of the Revolution in 1917: Vladimirovichi, Konstantinovichi, Nikolaevichi and Mikhailovichi. The book is illustrated with exquisite and rare photographs of these intriguing men, their families and descendants. It also includes several family trees. The chapters were authored by some of today's most recognized authors and scholars on the Romanov Dynasty. With a foreword by HRH Prince Michael of Kent.

The price of this hardback book is: USA price: $43.95 + shipping ($8 in the USA – $64.00 overseas). WE SHIP WORLDWIDE! To order by phone: (510) 236-1730 or email: books@eurohistory.com

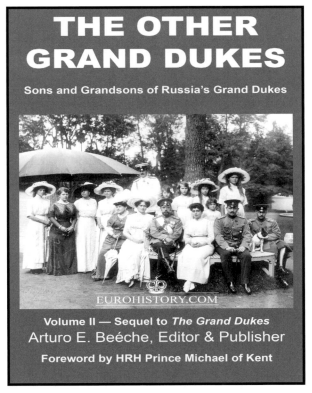

The Royal Hellenic Dynasty

This is the English-language version of Elleniki Dynazteia published in 2003. The book made an indelible impression on collectors of royal books back then. Due to its widespread acclaim, Eurohistory negotiated for the publication of the book in English as: The Royal Hellenic Dynasty, a book filled with more than 160 photographs of the Greek royal family from between 1863-1950. The Royal Hellenic Dynasty draws an exquisite selection of photos from the private collection of Mrs. Eleni Helmis-Markesinis. The captions were written by Prince Michael of Greece and translated by him and Arturo Beéche, Eurohistory's founder. The book is in the usual coffee-table format, hardback with dustjacket and printed in glossy paper.

Price: $29.95, plus shipping ($8.00 shipping and handling in the USA. International shipping and handling available for $26.00). To order by phone: (510) 236-1730 or email: books@eurohistory.com

APAPA: *King Christian IX of Denmark and His Descendants*

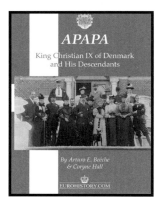

The history of King Christian IX of Denmark, the Father-in-law of Europe, and his descendants. Covering the last 150 years of the royal and imperial houses of: Denmark, Norway, Great Britain, Greece, Romania, Russia, Hanover, Baden, Mecklenburg-Schwerin and many other related dynasties and princely houses.

The authors have handsomely documented their writings with nearly 450 exquisite and rare photos of King Christian IX and his wife Louise and their descendants.

USA price: $48.95 plus shipping ($8.00 in the USA – $26.00 overseas). To order by phone: (510) 236-1730 or email: books@eurohistory.com

The Grand Duchesses

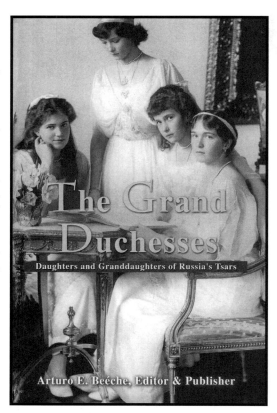

Eurohistory presents to you an amazing book about the daughters and granddaughters of Russia's Tsars from the time of Paul I.

Included in this unique work, are 26 biographies of Romanov women, along with exquisite and rare photographs — many of them from the private collections of Russia's Imperial Family.

The book also includes eight family trees, 36 glossy pages of beautiful photos of these women and their families — 73 photos in total, as well as contributions from many of today's most distinguished royalty authors.

The price of this paperback book is: USA price: $43.95 plus $8 shipping and handling. International shipping and handling: $26.00. To order by phone: (510) 236-1730 or email: books@eurohistory.com

Dear Ellen

Royal Europe Through the Photo Albums of Grand Duchess Helen Vladimirovna of Russia

Eurohistory is delighted to bring to you *Dear Ellen – Royal Europe Through the Photo Albums of Grand Duchess Helen Vladimirovna of Russia.*

With special access to the Grand Duchess' private photo albums, as well as images from the Eurohistory Archive and the private collections of the grand duchess' descendants, the author built a photographic journey covering the lives of Helen and her husband, Prince Nicholas of Greece. Also included are their three daughters: Olga of Yugoslavia, Elisabeth of Toerring-Jettenbach and Marina, Duchess of Kent. The selection of Romanov photos alone is phenomenal. The book also includes the galaxy of royalty in which the prince and his wife lived. Four of the grandchildren of Helen and Nicholas actively cooperated with the author bringing to light untold family stories and helping reconstruct the lives of two unique royal personages, now nearly forgotten.

Hardbound, glossy paper and contains more than 350 unique photographs, as well a massive several family tree showing Helen and Nicholas in the context of both their families. The book sells for $43.95 plus shipping ($8.00 in the USA – $26.00 overseas). Order by Phone: 510-236-1730 or email at: books@eurohistory.com

Royal Gatherings

Who is in the Picture? – Volume I

Inspired by a very popular feature inside the pages of EUROHISTORY, Ilana D. Miller and Arturo E. Beéche wrote a book on royal gatherings that happened between 1859-1914. Spanning many of Europe's royal families, Royal Gatherings tells the story behind 38 group photos of royals from King Francesco II of the Two Sicilies, to the wedding of Prince Heinrich of Prussia, and the Assassination of Archduke Franz Ferdinand of Austria.Royal Gatherings' 176 pages are filled with more than 250 unique photographs, most of them from the Eurohistory Archive and some from private royal collections.

The book sells for $43.95 plus shipping ($8.00 in the USA – $26.00 overseas). Order by Phone: 510-236-1730 or email at: books@eurohistory.com

Royal Gatherings

Who is in the Picture? – Volume II

Inspired by a very popular feature inside the pages of EUROHISTORY, Ilana D. Miller and Arturo E. Beéche wrote a book on royal gatherings that took place between 1914-1939. Spanning many of Europe's royal families, Royal Gatherings tells the story behind more than 30 group photos of royals from Nicholas II's last foreign visit to the wedding of the Duke of Spoleto, just before the start of WWII. Royal Gatherings' 240 pages are filled with more than 250 unique photographs, most of them from the Eurohistory Archive and some from private royal collections.

The book sells for $48.95 plus shipping ($8.00 in the USA – $26.00 overseas). Order by Phone: 510-236-1730 or email at: books@eurohistory.com

Maria Pia

Queen of Portugal

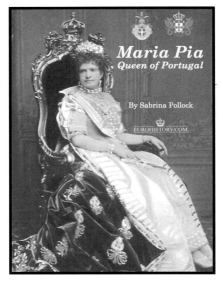

The first-ever biography of Portugal's controversial Queen Maria Pia, wife of King Luis, mother of assassinated King Carlos. Using previously unused sources, as well as the famed Queen's correspondence, the author managed to reconstruct the life of a strong woman who had a terribly difficult life in a kingdom where she arrived as a teen bride. A Savoy by birth, Maria Pia dedicated her life to the needs of her adopted country, Portugal.

Handsomely illustrated! The price of this hardback book is: USA price: $43.95 plus $8 shipping and handling. International shipping and handling: $26.00. To order by phone: (510) 236-1730 or email: books@ eurohistory.com

The Gotha – Volume I

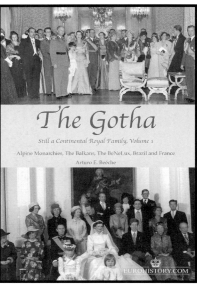

Since 1901 much has changed within the ranks of the Gotha and this study focuses on these changes. Mr. Beéche expertly analyzes these changes by studying the marriage alliances of thirteen ruling and formerly ruling dynasties: Albania, Austria-Hungary, Belgium, Brazil, Bulgaria, France (Napoléon and Orléans), Greece, Liechtenstein, Luxembourg, Montenegro, The Netherlands, Romania, & Yugoslavia. Relying on countless interviews with several royalties and experts, Mr. Beéche tells the candid story of how much the institution of royal marriage changed in the last century. This is the first in a multi-volume series that will cover all the houses in the Gotha's First Section. A must-have for the royal enthusiast!

It also contains 260+ unique photographs, as well as 25 family trees. The book sells for $43.95 plus shipping ($8.00 in the USA – $26.00 overseas).

The Russian Riddle

Grand Duke Serge Alexandrovich of Russia

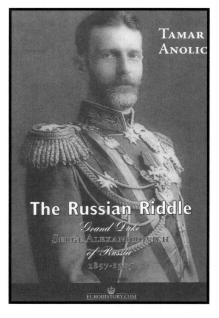

Tamar Anolic brings us a new approach, with a more human look, to the the historical figure of Grand Duke Serge Alexandrovich, one that looks at the man and not the myth. Son of Tsar Alexander II, brother of Alexander III and uncle of Nicholas II, as well as Governor General of Moscow, Serge played an important role in the affairs of Imperial Russia during the sunset of the Romanov dynasty.

Married to one of Europe's most beautiful princesses, Elisabeth of Hesse and by Rhine, his relationship with her led to others accusing Serge Alexandrovich of, what then were, unspeakable acts. His main detractor was the enigmatic, and troublesome, Kaiser Wilhelm II, who had been in love with Serge's wife. It is the very passionate story of a man much maligned, but who happened to be a loving husband and uncle, and a caring, dutiful and loyal son and brother.

The book sells for $43.95, Shipping: USA: $8.00, and International delivery: $26.00.